Julia Roth

Can Feminism Trump Populism?

Right-Wing Trends and Intersectional Contestations in the Americas

INTER-AMERICAN STUDIES
Cultures – Societies – History

ESTUDIOS INTERAMERICANOS
Culturas – Sociedades – Historia

Volume 28

Julia Roth

Can Feminism Trump Populism?

Right-Wing Trends and Intersectional Contestations in the Americas

Wissenschaftlicher Verlag Trier

Copublished by

UNO University of New Orleans Press

Can Feminism Trump Populism?
Right-Wing Trends and Intersectional Contestations in the Americas /
Julia Roth. –
(Inter-American Studies | Estudios Interamericanos; 28)
Trier: WVT Wissenschaftlicher Verlag Trier, 2021
ISBN 978-3-86821-821-3
New Orleans, LA: University of New Orleans Press, 2021
ISBN 978-1-60801-205-3

SPONSORED BY THE
Federal Ministry of Education and Research

The project, on which this book is based, has been funded by the German Federal Ministry of Education and Research (Bundesministerium für Bildung und Forschung, BMBF). The responsibility for the content of this publication lies with the author.

Cover Image: Pete Thompson / Gallery Stock
Cover Design: Brigitta Disseldorf

Library of Congress Cataloging-in-Publication Data
Names: Roth, Julia, author.
Title: Can feminism trump populism? : right-wing trends and intersectional contestations in the Americas / Julia Roth.
Description: Trier : Wissenschaftlicher Verlag ; New Orleans, LA : University of New Orleans Press, 2021. | Series: Inter-American studies: cultures, societies, history = Estudios interamericanos: culturas, sociedades, historia ; volume 28 | Includes bibliographical references.
Identifiers: LCCN 2020044323 | ISBN 9781608012053 (paperback)
Subjects: LCSH: Feminism--America. | Populism--America. | Right and left (Political science)--America.
Classification: LCC HQ1400 .R68 2021 | DDC 305.420973--dc23
LC record available at https://lccn.loc.gov/2020044323

Publisher: WVT Wissenschaftlicher Verlag Trier, Postfach 4005, D-54230 Trier, Bergstraße 27, D-54295 Trier, Tel. 0049 651 41503, Fax 41504, www.wvttrier.de, wvt@wvttrier.de

Copublisher: University of New Orleans Press, 2000 Lakeshore Drive, Earl K. Long Library, Room 221, New Orleans, LA 70148, United States, 504-280-7457, unopress.org

To Polly Luz, the next generation.

For the people hear us singing:
Bread and roses, bread and roses.

Table of Contents

Part I

1. Right-Wing Populist Gains and Feminist Contestations

1.1. Right-Wing Populist Gains

Photo no. 1: Palácio do Planalto. Meeting of Jair Bolsonaro and Donald Trump – exchange of shirts. March, 2019. Wikimedia Commons.

Shortly before the presidential elections in the US in October 2016, Republican candidate Donald Trump hit the headlines with a video from 2005 in which he made sexist comments in an interview to television host Billy Bush. In the video now known as the "Access Hollywood Tape", Trump boasts about his power over women and refers to his practices of sexually assaulting them ("grab them by the pussy"). The video was published by the Washington Post, causing outrage in the public debate, though reactions among Republicans varied. This outrage notwithstanding, Donald Trump was shortly afterwards elected as 45th president of the United States of America. After his election, Trump was accused of numerous further cases of sexual assault, none of which has until now seriously harmed him.

During the 2018 electoral campaign in Brazil, Jair Messias Bolsonaro, presidential candidate of the right-wing party *Partido Social Liberal* (PSL) also made the headlines with sexist remarks. One of his most often cited comments is the one he made to federal deputy Maria do Rosário at the Chamber of Deputies in 2003, stating that he would never rape her, because she doesn't deserve it (McLoughlin 2019). Bolsonaro is also quoted as having claimed that he had a daughter "in a moment of weakness" after four sons, and numerous of his comments were seen to justify the gender pay gap and sexism or included openly homophobic and racist remarks (Uchoa 2018). Not surprisingly, the media soon referred to Bolsonaro as "Brazil's Trump" (McLoughlin 2019) or "Tropical Trump" (The Daily Mail 2018). Regardless of such openly hostile remarks, Bolsonaro was elected president in the second ballot in October 2018, taking office on January 1, 2019. When Bolsonaro visited Trump in the US on March 19, 2019, he emphasized their common struggle as being against "political correctness", "fake news", and "the gender ideology."

1.2. Feminist Contestations

As US president Donald Trump's inauguration was celebrated on January 21, 2016, 700,000 people participated in the "Women's March" in Washington, among them many celebrities, ranging from civil rights activists Angela Davis to Democrat Bernie Sanders and film maker Michael Moore, from pop singer Madonna to actresses America Ferrera and Scarlett Johansson and singer songwriter and actress Janelle Monáe. More than one million marched all over the United States, and 670 demonstrations were organized globally (see 'The Women's March' website www.womensmarch.com and The Women's March Organizers and Condé Nast 2018, WMO in the following). Under the hashtag #NotMyPresident, people all over the US soon united to oppose Trump's election, and February 20, 2017 was even called "Not My Presidents Day". Since then, the movement has developed into a yearly event, as the mobilizations in January

2019 have shown. In November 2017, the Women's March organizers launched the first National Women's Conference in Houston in 40 years, and many followers fight against racist, sexist and homophobic violence and have engaged in grassroots movements to nominate other candidates for the 2018 midterm and 2020 federal elections. Many took part in the International Women's Strikes on March 8.

Jair Bolsonaro's election campaign in Brazil was also accompanied by broad feminist resistance (see Darlington 2018). Under the banner *#EleNão* (#NotHim) and *#MulheresContraBolsonaro* (Women Against Bolsonaro), above all Afro-Brazilian feminists mobilized immense protests online and in the streets against this openly sexist, misogynist, homophobic, and racist candidate. The weekend before the first round of elections on October 7, tens of thousands of people joined marches across the country in the biggest female organized street demonstration in Brazilian history (Kaiser 2018). Marches were organized also in other major cities worldwide, among them Lisbon, London and Berlin under the banner "*#EleNão* – Brazilians against Fascism" (see *#EleNão*). A forceful feminist countermovement had begun to take shape after the assassination of the openly gay Afro-Brazilian politician Marielle Franco in March 2018 under the slogan *Marielle presente!* (Marielle [is] present) and now forms part of a wider movement against sexual harassment, sexism and discrimination. The recent Women's Strikes took the protests a step further.

Photo no. 2: Mobilus In Mobili. Women's March on Washington. January 2017. Flickr.

Photo no. 3: Brasil de Fato. Women in Milan, Italy in protest against Bolsonaro. September 2018. Flickr.

1.3. Right-Wing Trends

Both the election of two openly misogynist and sexist presidents and the protests their success provoked indicate a cultural(ized) struggle over power, representation and definition, as well as over diversity and solidarity, is in full swing. And gender – or, rather, the denunciation of the gender concept and feminism – is one of the central arenas in which this struggle is being carried out. Birgit Sauer emphasizes that while gender ideologies have always been important for right-wing actors, “only recently has a gender-based strategy moved to the forefront of (…) right-wing populist actors” (2017, 1, translation JR). Trump and Boslonaro oppose the affirmative action policies their predecessors introduced and supported, and both politicians also take a stance against sexual diversity in education. Furthermore, both attacked their female predecessor or competitor – Hillary Clinton and Dilma Rousseff respectively – and thereby tried to play down and ridicule the first women who claimed the highest office. Simultaneously, however, both Donald Trump and Jair Bolsonaro mobilized female supporters for their cause, apparently aware that this could be a strategically useful and necessary move in the current constellation. The right-wing populist presidential candidates make acceptable a regressive racist and sexist discourse that also infiltrates other political social forces. It is notable that these struggles center around gender, even though gender is interpellated in very different ways. Trump and Bolsonaro serve as extreme exemplary cases for broader circumstances that go beyond their public personas and presidencies, hinting at tendencies and transformations that numerous societies are currently facing in the light of neoliberal precarization and crisis.

This study will thus – mainly, but not exclusively – focus on these two individual cases in order to discuss the similar patterns and respective differences that can be observed as a culmination or indicator of current trends. The research this study is based on was conducted between 2017 and 2019. Even though the political landscape has slightly changed since then – while finishing these lines, Joe Biden was about to be inaugurated to replace Donald Trump as president of the US – the phenomenon of right-wing nationalism prevails and gains strength, and related patterns of gendering remain highly relevant in order to understand the phenomenon. The epistemological scene of gender thus currently – once again – constitutes an (open) "battlefield" and a fundamental intervention into the public discussion. This is why a systematic discussion of the ways in which gender provides an arena for right-wing populist agendas, but also for resistance and emancipatory counter-narratives, is so timely and urgent. The current study aims to be an intervention into this newly emerging field. It seeks to bring together existent approaches and voices, contributing to a first overview and to the development of a toolbox for analyzing how right-wing populism articulates discourses using gender.

1.4. Some First Notes on Populism

In the course of the recent rise in right-wing populism, the gender(ed) politics of right-wing populist actors are articulated in very different ways, and it is illuminating to compare particular strategies. In central and northern Europe, some variations of progressive gender politics are included into – and, often times appropriated by – populist parties, whereas in East European countries populists are opposed to feminist and gender-political positions. This can be observed in recent political activity against the right to legal abortion (in Poland) or for the abolishment of academic Gender Studies (in Hungary). At the same time, many populist parties present high-profile female leadership figures, and some don't oppose (or even represent?) alternative gender/family models. So, we can see several dynamic paradoxes taking place at the same time. In the USA and Brazil, we see not as many female leadership figures – Trump has had Sarah Sanders, Hope Hicks, Kierstjen Nielsen, Nikki Haley, Betsey DeVos, Gina Haspel, Omarosa Manigault, and, of course, Ivanka and Bolsonaro his current minister for family Damares Alves etc. – and feminism is mostly discussed in opposition to Trumpism or Bolsonaro's politics.

The Americas in particular provide a good case study for delineating major trends or strands of the entanglements between right-wing populism and gender. On the one hand, many studies situate the origin of populism (at least as a mass phenomenon – populist movements can already be observed in the 19th century in the US and East Europe – see Mudde and Kaltwasser 2017) in the Latin American context, most of them viewing *Peronismo* in Argentina as model example. The role of Evita Perón for the success of *Peronismo* particularly among the female electorate indicates the crucial role of gender for populist logics. On the other hand, current examples of populist actors in parts of the Americas – e.g. in Brazil and the USA – point to different facets, but also to structural similarities of context-bound populisms.

The field of research in right-wing populism is now quite established and is expanding very quickly (see e.g. Taggart 2000, Canovan 2002, Laclau 2005, Mudde and Kaltwasser 2013). Some notions such as populist Zeitgeist, thin ideology (Mudde 2004), illiberal democracy (Zakaria 1997), and observations such as a special gender gap in voting behavior have now become common knowledge. However, while the worldwide rise of right-wing populist parties and leaders, of anti-pluralism, anti-elitism and anti-genderism has led to a proliferation in theorizing on populism, the function of gender in and for populism "remains largely understudied", as Sahar Abi-Hassan (2017) claims in her contribution to the Oxford Handbook on Populism. (Abi-Hassan mentions Kampwirth 2010 and Spierings and Zaslove 2015 as exceptions.)

This study focuses on the relationship between the two fields, based on the assumption that a gender focus on populism will not only enrich the study field, but can provide an innovative parameter for a re-evaluation of the phenomenon and the theorizing on (right-wing) populism. The study thus pursues a two-fold aim: first, to examine the logic and function of gender for (right-wing) populism in order to re-evaluate the phenomenon and expand the theorizing towards more complex forms of descriptions and analysis, and, secondly, to sketch out spaces and practices of resistance that are also based on gendered politics (or, make resistance to anti-sexism their point of departure). Based on the observation of the simultaneous emergence of strong feminist movements in many places where a strong right-wing populist trend can be observed, the study recognizes gender, anti-sexism and intersectional feminism as a means of contestation and resistance to right-wing populist and similar new conservative and fundamentalist forces, aiming to provide a first outline for further elaborations on the interactions between right-wing populism and gender.

Focusing on the role that gender plays in populist discourses (and populism is currently not only radicalized but also gendered in a particular way) brings some of the core specificities of current populism logics into view. From a European perspective, where anti-genderism ranges from more "covert" and complex entanglements between gender and right-wing populism (Kuhar and Paternotte 2017) – from outright hostile positions found in Poland or Hungary to positions that underscore the own culture's superiority in order to promote culturalist-racist anti-Muslim migration defense like in Germany, Austria or the Netherlands – the study examines how gendered rhetorics function in the Brazilian and US contexts. As the introductory examples indicate, populist discourse is more openly sexist and racist in these countries. In all cases "genderism" (and, partly, "feminism") is constructed as an inner enemy of the "pure people" / the autochthonous population / the average man (and woman) while the "own" culture is praised as more civilized and emancipated, also based on arguments related to gender, race, and sexual politics as discursive weapons in the struggle over cultural hegemony. Gayle Rubin's (1984) has argued that sexuality is often the battleground of other social conflicts, in the form of "moral panics", which conservative forces mobilize in order to undermine liberal achievements, for "displacing social anxieties", and "discharging their attendant emotional intensity" (267). Building on Rubin, Gabriele Dietze's work includes not only the intersection of sexuality and gender but also the intersection with race (2017, 17). The study asks how populist actors communicate social-political and cultural topics via gender and why gender seemingly provides a particularly suitable platform for bringing issues such as demography, anti-immigration, national belonging and citizenship, (re)distribution etc. into the public arena.

Gender norms and gender relations were also one of the battlefields of anti-discrimination and anti-hegemony in the 1960s and 1970s, and it is in this field that numerous successes were achieved, ranging from the integration of more women into the labor market to a greater variety of family models and sexual diversity. Through the success of the emancipatory social movements of the 20th century – also known as "sexual revolution" – traditional gender hierarchies and orders have been challenged and transformed towards much more diverse societies. It is therefore no coincidence that gender is now once again evoked as a framework for a variety of topics, particularly by right-wing populists and conservative Catholics, Evangelicals, or Pentecostals.

Right-wing populist parties consider family and reproductive politics as a key epistemological arena of policy and are strongly influenced by conservative Christian conceptions of morals and ethics as well as by Catholic and Protestant fundamentalisms. However, it is not enough to reduce these phenomena and observation to a mere conservative misogynist backlash, since the ways in which right-wing populist logics and discourse are entangled with gender ideas is more complex and multi-layered. For the self-conception of populist actors and parties, traditional gender orders and the heteronormative nuclear family play a pivotal role, as can be increasingly observed in a wave of so-called "anti-genderism" campaigns in Europe and the Americas (Colombia, Brazil), anti-affirmative action campaigns (USA, Brazil), and various attempts to prevent or withdraw the right to abortion (Argentina, USA) or campaigns against homosexuals and transgender persons (Brazil). In contradiction to this major trend, we see both in Europe and, to a certain degree, in the USA a form of "sexual nationalism" (Mepschen and Duyvendak 2012) which highlights the presumed sexual emancipation of the "legitimate" inhabitants via the narrative of the sexual backwardness of Muslim immigrants, refugees, Africans, or afro-descendant (and, in the Americas, indigenous) parts of the population. Some of these trends are met by a certain "emancipation fatigue" (Dietze 2019) by women who feel exhausted by the ongoing pressure to "manage it all", while the gendered division of labor prevails. Understood as a "practice of interpellation" (Stegemann 2017, 41), that caters to different communication styles depending on the historical and political situation, populism for right-wing actors can thus function as a relief or unloading. As this study will show, gender provides a fundamental dimension for this interpellative logic, particularly also in media discourses by or about popular actors. This is a logic that is highly compatible with the logics of mass (and, increasingly, social) media. According to Stegemann (2017), right-wing populist hatred is directed towards the liberal world and its political and cultural values, and overshadows an analysis of the (neo)liberal economy and the inequalities related to it (131). By transferring economic and global inequalities and hierarchies to the – established binary – gender hierarchy, they are naturalized and thus attached to received (gendered and racialized) narratives and imaginaries of belonging. If gender serves as a decisive platform to communicate and negotiate right-wing populist aims, as this study asserts, is it from gender and feminist perspectives/positions that resistance and counter-narratives can effectively emerge?

Assuming that the current protests point to the potential of anti-sexism for uniting strategic alliances against right-wing populism, the second part of this study examines the ways in which current feminist movements defining themselves as "intersectional" serve as a socio-political force against the recent right-wing conservative and populist trend and the neoliberalization and de-solidarization of broad parts of societies all over the Americas (and the world). Following Judith Butler's book *Notes Toward a Performative Theory of Assembly* (2015), in the second part on new feminist movements, this study asks whether and under what conditions current intersectional feminist movements are able to enact forms of radical solidarity. The second part examines the ways in which current movements perform “embodied ways of coming together”, in opposition to destructive political and economic forces and create a new sense of “the people” as interdependent, beyond the exclusionary logics of right-wing populism, and thus, of public space and democracy/sociability. Regarding the contemporary scenario of feminist movements in the context of right-wing populist politics in the Americas, we see how feminism/gender functions as a platform for resistance and counter-narratives to the described right-wing populism tendencies and what possible effects they (can) have.

In a historical excursus into the long experience with manifold axes of inequality and resistance in the Americas, this study then asks whether this history has led to a special sensitization for “intersectionalities” (see e.g. Shepherd 2008 and 2011, Shepherd, Brereton, Bailey 1995, dos Santos 2007). The recent “intersectional” feminisms in the Americas call back to centuries of confronting and interrogating interlocking axes of oppression, mainly by marginalized voices, groups and social movements. Thus, in a second step, this study sheds light on the revitalized feminist movements in Argentina, Chile and Brazil, Mexico and the US, which follow an increasingly “intersectional” politics in order to counter the sexist, racist, homophobic backlash.

Finally, the study discusses the commonalities and differences, the boundaries and possibilities of the strategies and programs of the new movements as discursive, epistemic, and political counter spaces to the increasing backlashes of patriarchal and racist actors and politics based on recent publications (books, blogs, websites, videos) and interviews with representatives of singular movements (Women’s March in San Francisco and New York, *Ni Una Menos* in Argentina, and feminist activists from Brazil). In what ways does the long experience of feminist confrontation in the Americas provide today’s feminisms with the tools for opposing current conservative and right-wing streams? To what degree can intersectional feminist movements contribute to thinking, imagining, and creating other forms of the social?

2. Trajectories and Definitions of Populism

2.1. Early Populists in the USA

Generally, populism can be seen as a modern phenomenon, emerging in the USA and Russia in the 19th century. Populism has been most prevalent in the democracies of Europe and the Americas, where it has been expressed in very heterogeneous ways: left or right, conservative or progressive, religious or secular. The long history of populist mobilization started with agrarian revolts giving rise to economic and social transitions, and early forms were marked by their spontaneous emergence. From the early prairie populists in the 19th century to the Occupy and Tea Party movements, US populisms have further been marked by their rather regional mobilization and the weak level of organization/institutionalization (Mudde and Kaltwasser 2017, 22-23). At the end of the 19th century and early 20th century in the United States, infrastructural transitions such as the extension of the railroad system and economic transformations affected rural areas in particular. Against this backdrop, so-called "prairie populists" viewed the free and independent farmers of European descent as "the people", in opposition to an "elite" of bankers and politicians in the North who produced nothing. While those early forms disappeared at the beginning of the 20th century, populism theorists Cass Mudde and Cristóbal Rovira Kaltwasser (2017) see populism's return "with a vengeance" (24) during the Cold War period, particularly in form of the right-wing mass movements against the thread of left-wing ideas. Communism and fascism, according to Mudde and Kaltwasser (2017), even though they "flirted with populism", are more elitist than populist, since they exalted the leader and 'race' (or the state or party) rather than the people (33). In this context, in the US, the common and ("real") patriotic Americans from the heartland constituted "the people", while "the elite" in the (Northeast) coastal areas supported "un-American" socialist ideas and promoted the re-distribution of wealth to an undeserving non-white underclass. The radicalized dimension becomes particularly obvious here, since "the people" are squeezed between a corrupt elite and a racialized underclass (24). In the 1960s, the notion of the "enemy within" changed from communists to civil rights activists, and in the 1970s to "activist judges" and academics. The narrative shifted toward the imaginary of the "American way of life" being attacked from the inside by a "liberal elite" – embodied by feminists and affirmative action supporters – who supported costly welfare state measures and granted "special privileges" to undeserving minorities (25). Migrants are constructed as a threat to the heartland's wealth, lifestyle and security from the outside. This is particularly apparent since the Homeland Security Act implemented after the terror attacks of September 11, 2001 (e.g. in form of the Tea Party movement within the Republican Party or the openly racist Alt-Right), or the way Venezuelan refugees are depicted in Brazilian media.

2.2. Populism in Latin America

Latin America is for Mudde and Kaltwasser (2017, 27) the region with the "most enduring prevalent tradition" of populism, due to the region's high levels of socioeconomic inequalities and the relatively long periods of democratic rule. Populist narratives address the concentration of the economic and political power in the hands of a small minority, an oligarchy that acts against the will of the people. Consequently, there is great support for populist movements that promise to do away with the rule of oligarchies and install governments in which the people rule themselves. Therefore, Latin American populisms have tended to be organized "from below", and thus inclusionary, giving voice to the formerly marginalized. For the Latin American context, Mudde and Kaltwasser (2013) make out three "waves" of populism. They situate the first "wave" from the Great Depression of the 1920s until the 1960s, when in many Latin American countries such as Ecuador, Chile or Argentina, populism became more successful than communism or socialism in the face of urbanization and the demand for rights. The populist rhetoric of this phase focused on "the people" (rather than on the working class), consisting of a "virtuous" community of peasants and workers of European descent while excluding afro-descendant and indigenous citizens. Moreover, characterizing the national oligarchy, in alliance with imperial forces, as "the corrupt elite", Latin American populists of this phase relied on a common identity against the interference of imperial powers which Mudde and Kaltwasser (2013) call an "ideology of *Americanismo*".

The second phase of populisms in Latin America starts in the early 1980s after the economic crises in Argentina, followed by Carlos Menem's government (1989-1999), in Brazil with the presidency of Fernando Color de Mello (1990-1992), and in Peru with Alberto Fujimori (1990-2000). These populist leaders blamed the elite for the dramatic economic situation and for robbing the people of their rightful sovereignty. They had no clear programmatic direction, but implemented blatant neoliberal reforms in cooperation with multinational institutions such as the IMF, as well as installing anti-poverty programs. The people were seen more as a passive mass than active citizens, and a common identity of *Americanismo* no longer played a major role.

The third wave of populism in Latin America – also known as the *Pink Tide* – starts in 1998 with the election of Hugo Chávez (1999-2013) as president of Venezuela, followed by Evo Morales (since 2006) in Bolivia, Rafael Correa (2007-2017) in Ecuador and Daniel Ortega in Nicaragua (since 2007). These populist leaders once again made use of anti-imperialist rhetoric and a resistant *Americanismo* identity. As a reaction to the prior neoliberal reforms of the second wave, they combine populist ideas with socialist ones, as can be observed in their parties' names. However, all of them must also act within the logics of neoliberal capitalist economies in countries that, due to a long history of colonial exploitation, are to a high degree dependent on resource extraction and export (see Coronil 2011). Lena Lavinas (2017) also emphasizes the crucial role of these countries' dependence on the export of resources, particularly the role of extractivism (economies depending on the extraction of primary resources to be sold on the world market) and multinational companies:

> And what exactly happened to Latin America during the Pink Tide? For most leftist and center-left governments, including Brazil and Argentina, there was a shift to reprimarization of the economy, marking a return to extractivism rather than deploying more audacious development strategies that would take time to mature but which would have finally fueled that structural shift which we have been expecting for decades. (Lavinas 2017)

Against the backdrop of such persistent colonial inequalities as expressed in the dependency of resource extractivism, "the people" are hence discursively constituted of all those who are discriminated against, marginalized and excluded. Most of the second wave leaders also opted for a constitutional assembly designed to constrain the capacities of the opposition, and thus, the plurality of voices and viewpoints. Looking particularly at Nicolás Maduro in Venezuela or Jair Bolsonaro in Brazil, Lavinas sees a submission to the "desire to remain in power" (or, one might add gain power) in the current Latin American versions of populism, especially in the context of the current neoliberal backlash. The examples of Nicolás Maduro in Venezuela, Daniel Ortega in Nicaragua, and Jair Bolsonaro in Brazil show that the general notion of Latin American populism(s) as emerging "from below" and as inclusionary is also shifting. Since the so-called Pink Tide, i.e., the turn to the left of many Latin American countries, is considerably weakened, a fourth phase might include these new trends.

2.3. Populist Trajectories in Europe

The first populist movements in Europe can be traced back to the agrarian uprisings in Russia and Eastern Europe, such as the narodniki or the "Go to the People movement" in Russia, whose influence remained limited as they were excluded from political power (Mudde and Kaltwasser 2017, 32). As mentioned, communism –

like fascism – "flirted" with populism, but Mudde and Kaltwasser (2017) define both as more elitist than populist (33). Only in the 1990s do they see the (re-)emergence of populism as a relevant political force in Europe. Most populist actors of this current phase combine populism with nativist and authoritarian ideologies, basing their political demands on a politics of "law and order" and a xenophobic antagonism between "the nation" and "aliens", neoliberal economics and a decidedly anti-elite posture. Examples of such new populist actors are the Front National in France, the Forza Italia in Italy, the UKIP promoting Brexit in the UK, the FPÖ in Austria, or the AfD in Germany. In Eastern Europe, according to Mudde and Kaltwasser (2017), many parties follow a discourse of the "stolen revolution" and promise to complete the unfulfilled revolution of 1989 – which was also based on the slogan "we are the people". While most populist movements have been rather right-wing oriented, the so-called Great Recession of 2008-2011 also brought about a momentum of left-wing populism such as the *Indignados* and *Podemos* in Spain or the radical left *Syriza* coalition in Greece, who stand for a Euroskeptic position and condemn the EU's austerity measures.

2.4. Populism and Democracy versus Authoritarianism

Populism can be democratic as well as authoritarian. While most populists are highly critical of conventional forms of institutionalized political representation such as parties, they usually share a demand for more direct democracy. Authoritarian forms instead focus more on a charismatic leader. Populism theorists Mudde and Kaltwasser (2017) even characterize populism as "one of the buzzwords of the 21st century", describing the phenomenon as broad and widespread. Underscoring the vagueness of the term and the contested nature of the concept, and also warning of its use as a battle term, Mudde and Kaltwasser situate (contemporary) populism(s) in the framework of liberal democracies. Due to this oscillation of content and the lack of a consistent program, populism has been conceptualized as a 'thin centered ideology' (Mudde and Kaltwasser

2017, 6), to which diverse projects, convictions, and attitudes can cling and connect. While they see populism as theoretically juxtaposed to (liberal) democracy, empirically most populist actors mobilize within liberal democratic frameworks. They argue that populism profits from the democratic idea of the general will of the people, whom most populist actors claim to represent, as well as from the possibilities of electoral democracies and the disappointments with (neo)liberal democracy. "The people", "the elite", and "the general will" of the people that is denied by corrupt elites and that the populists stand for, form the core concepts of populist discourse, around which further populist concepts can build. The general construction of the antagonism between "the (pure) people" versus "the (corrupt) elite" helps populism to serve as a sort of mental map to analyze and comprehend reality. Usually, populist narratives present the corrupt ruling elite as working against the "will of the people" and, in right-wing populism, in favor of a non-white underclass to whom the elite undeservingly distributes what belongs to the people. Research has revealed right-wing populists' double antagonism, in which "the people" is constructed "vertically" as "ordinary people" opposed to the elite (Ajanovic, Mayer and Sauer 2018, cf. Canovan 1999, 5) and "horizontally', positioned against 'the others". In right-wing populist discourses 'the people' turn into "our people" (Ajanovic, Mayer and Sauer 2018) thus putting national belonging and non-belonging on center stage. In doing so, right-wing populism invokes both of these antagonistic traditions and capitalizes on the tensions that arise from them (Ajanovic, Mayer and Sauer 2018, 637).

Donald Trump and Jair Bolsonaro seem to be following the Manichean worldview ascribed to populism, based on the narrative of the "betrayed people". Both Trump and Bolsonaro increased their visibility and "shock value" as presidential candidates through openly sexist, misogynist, racist, and, in Bolsonaro's case in particular, homophobic statements. This happened in the current climate in which right-wing actors and parties are on the rise worldwide. If one considers their politics as – at least partly – following a populist logic, their success is not surprising.

While right-wing populism tends to be exclusionary, based on a narrowly ethnic notion of "the people", Latin American populism has generally been inclusive in character, basing its understanding of "the people" on the excluded (Mudde and Kaltwasser 2013). However, as we can see in current developments in Brazil and other places, such clear-cut divisions seem no longer to hold true, if we look for instance at figures such as Jair Bolsonaro and Bernie Sanders. Sanders has been considered as left-wing populist by many, while Bolsonaro represents a Latin American right-wing populist leader. These regional specificities seem to be shifting, and the respective concepts may need to be expanded or adapted. Moreover, regional phenomena can create similar populist actors such as right-wing parties in Europe and radical left populists in Latin America (Mudde and Kaltwasser 2017, 21). A common feature can be observed in all current versions of right-wing populism: an 'obsession with gender' and sexuality in different arenas (see Dietze and Roth 2020, 7). In many cases, gender serves these actors as a platform for the struggle over values and the distribution of resources, since gendered notions of family and nation are closely linked to understandings of democracy.

In the following, I will thus present five (communicative) patterns relating to gender on which current right-wing populist discourse builds, using gender as a discursive and epistemic platform.

3. Five Right-Wing Populist Patterns of En-Gendering

During his first visit to Washington on March 19, 2019, Jair Bolsonaro created headlines by stating that he stands united with Donald Trump to ensure liberties and traditional family lifestyles with "respect to God our creator" and "against the gender ideology" – in the face of "the politically correct attitudes" and "fake news" (Goldberg 2019). The common points he emphasized – religious values, the opposition to gender approaches and political correctness, and to the "fake news" represented by mainstream media, seem to be no coincidence. The crucial role he ascribes to anti-genderism, the struggle against non-discriminatory language and against mainstream media in the name of conservative religious values tie in very nicely with the systemic logic of populism. Bolsonaro also employs the notion of a "war" about cultural hegemony in light of the post-1968 diversification of family models and gender identities, which have begun to de-center White heteronormative patriarchal masculinity.

Populism research has heretofore neither put the gender question and related sexual-political strategies center stage in a systematic manner, nor acknowledged the epistemic value of gender as a meta allegory for very different dynamics. In her pioneering 2017 article, Birgit Sauer emphasizes the ways in which gender provides ample metaphoric material, since gender is a category that usually evokes emotional responses. Gender tackles everyday experiences that everyone can relate to, and because everyone is gendered in a certain way. Sauer ascribes to gender a crucial role for the "jointing of a national-populist project of ethnic or national homogeneity and exclusionary citizenship in the biopolitical arrangements" (Sauer 2017, 14, translation JR) of the new right. Dietze and Roth thus postulate an 'obsession with gender' and sexuality in different arenas as a common feature that can be observed in all current versions of right-wing populism (Dietze and Roth 2020, 7). In right-wing populism these are related to a long tradition of nativist right-wing discourse centering on the (right/White) female body as guarantor for the maintenance of the nation. In her analysis of gender for the establishing and maintenance of global inequalities as a condition of possibility for capitalism and the related structures that enabled to "transfer the cost of reproduction of wage-workers from capitalist enterprise or state to the household", Manuela Boatcă describes the respective subordination and exclusion of women via naturalized social categories as "gendering as defining-into-nature" (2015, 73). In her critical study on anti-gender politics of rightwing parties, Juliane Lang already interpreted these "gendered and sexual normatives" as attempts of a "(re-)production of the national (*völkisch*) order", and thus pleaded for "an entanglement of right-wing extremism and gender research" (Lang 2013, 94).

The above-mentioned examples from Trump's and Bolsonaro's presidential campaigns have shown how both candidates, while making openly sexist and racist remarks, simultaneously were able to mobilize voters and supporters through seemingly feminist/women's rights topics such as the protection of women's sexual freedom. Those examples indicate how much populist actors in the Americas manage to polarize their societies through gender-related topics, but also that they gain approval for re-energizing debates about immigration control, demography, abortion, or well-fare in the public sphere.

As the examples from the US and Brazil show – the tendencies of which we can also observe in other parts of the world, particularly in Northern Europe – discourses on gender thus become part of the Manichean worldview right-wing populist logics are built on, and which require the creation of antagonisms in order to function. Gender thus serves as an arena for the polarizations that stem from the developments resulting from the anti-hegemonic projects following the social movements of the 1960s and 1970s which are revived in the current climate of neoliberal competitions for resources. The right-wing populist and conservative opposition to these developments are increasingly expressed through so-called "anti-genderism", the demonization of social constructivist gender studies approaches and women's and LGBTQI equality rights activism in favor of abortion rights and sexual diversity. A growing number of women supporting right-wing populism express their rejection of what they consider feminism's or gender ideology's destruction of traditional gender roles and attack on family values, as well as the pressure to work full-time and educate children about sexual diversity. While "genderism" thus functions as one of the "inner enemies" of right-wing populist logic (together with "the (corrupt) elite" of which feminists form part), women's (and gays') rights and sexual freedom are often used as an argument against the "intruding" enemy of immigrants and refugees who are constructed as a sexual threat. Moreover, for an increasingly strong transnational network of right-wing radicals, gender serves as a language to attack neoliberalism (and global capitalism) by depicting "gender ideology" as a means of colonization. As this study will show, examining the "communicative patterns" or "schemes" that can currently be observed in radical right and right-wing populist discourse, sheds light onto how these practices and politics are intrinsically "gendered". In relation to the right-wing populist logic, different patterns of gendering serve different functions along the following lines:

- Pattern I: Gender as "Affective Bridge" in Mass Media (Gendering of scandals + Others)
- Pattern II: Appropriating Women's Politics for Femonationalist Arrangements
- Pattern III: (White) Re-Masculinization: "Genderism" as Existential Threat
- Pattern IV: Reverse Anti-Colonialism: "Gender Ideology" as "Ideological Colonization", Radical Religious and Femoglobal Alliances
- Pattern IV: "Ethno-sexism" and "Exclusive Intersectionality" (Gendering of Social Inequalities and Gendering of Fear).

3.1. Pattern I: Gender as "Affective Bridge" in (Mass) Media

Besides "gender ideology" and "political correctness", a further important marker of commonality for Jair Bolsonaro during his visit to

Donald Trump in March 2019 was their shared opposition to and fight against "fake news".

Understood as a "political logic" (Laclau 2005, 117) and a "communicative scheme" (Stegemann 2017, 22) or "communicative pattern" (Costa 2018), right-wing populism gains from its entanglements with the workings of mass media. Current right-wing populists offer a new, or revived, exclusionary narrative, often purporting to be saying "what everyone was thinking", and "shunning the politically correct" – referring to language policies that are perceived as excessive or unwarranted in conservative criticism of the New Left. The media is usually condemned as the enemy, even as populist actors depend on media and take advantage of the shared logics of populism and media regarding attention economies and emotionality (see Diehl 2017). Not surprisingly, the success of current populist actors is discussed in relation to mass media, and increasingly in relation with the ever more important role of social media. For both Trump and Bolsonaro as candidates – and later as presidents – the role of mass media has been crucial. Shunning the 'politically correct' forms a central part of their populist strategy of condemning "the elite" of media, politicians and intellectual left-wingers, as their crusade against "fake news" illustrates. Mass media, in turn, also follow the logic that "sex sells" and often use sexual politics and gender topics in order to gain attention through scandal and appealing to affective reactions.

Paula Diehl (2017) examines the strong appeal populists find in mass media and points out that populism and mass media are marked by a number of parallel logics. Populists embody characteristics that meet the attention economy and the rules and criteria of mass media by creating scandals, breaking taboos, and appealing to emotions. Like mass media, populist leaders rely on promising more participation. As Diehl shows, mass media serve to catapult right-wing extremist positions into the public sphere. The danger lies in the fact that the media, through their constant repetition, contribute to the normalization of such positions and eventually to a shift towards non-democratic and even anti-democratic standards. Gender plays a crucial role in this respect since "sex and blood" always helps to fulfill the attention logics of media, and gender issues appeal to the everyday and to everyone, thus guaranteeing a certain affective engagement by all recipients. Gender moreover builds on a long established naturalized hierarchical binary. Gender applies to numerous logics of right-wing populism and serves various populist communicative patterns. Right-wing populism works against gender-sensitive "politically correct" language and contributes to the normalization of sexist and racist language. The crucial role of gender for the construction of feminism and gender ideology as "inner enemies" in the binary populist logic and the dynamic paradoxes created by populist actors' alliances with certain women and seemingly feminist arguments while reviving hegemonic masculinity has been a neglected aspect in populism research. It will be the focus of the patterns examined below. The fact that the new populists know now that they need to present a more modernized image and depend on the support of women (and, partly, representatives of LGBTQI and other marginalized communities) and consciously include and use the voices of female voters and supporters, shows how crucial gender has become for negotiating a broad range of topics. This trend also indicates that more is at stake than a backlash or return to traditional roles.

The electoral campaigns of both Donald Trump and Jair Bolsonaro have shown that mass media increasingly play a major role in their strategies to directly spread their messages to their followers, who are, however no longer (only) the "masses" of TV times, but increasingly also carefully targeted Twitter, Facebook and WhatsApp users. Via social media, they aim at direct communication between the leader or party and their followers, since communication from a populist view needs to be unmediated. Social media facilitate this logic and therefore play an increasingly important role in election campaigns and political communication of populists, as can currently be observed in Bolsonaro's successful WhatsApp and YouTube electoral campaign and Trumps constant interventions via Twitter, which are frequently quoted by media of all sorts.

Following Diehl, through the "systemic affinity" of populism and mass media, populists get more media attention than other political actors, while populists often use the attention rules of mass media as part of a clear strategy to gain attention and, eventually, votes. These media also serve the populist actors' strategy of contradicting "mainstream" media and declaring their version of events to be "wrong" or "fake". At the same time, they constantly cause distraction, controversies, dramatization, and scandal, which ties in with mass media's and social media's attention logics. The examples of the openly sexist remarks of Trump and Bolsonaro at the beginning of this study show how these populist actors tend to make statements for their shock value and consciously and repeatedly cause scandals. Gender topics are particularly useful here, due to their "sex sells" logic and their affective appeal. Through their direct communication with their voters through Twitter, WhatsApp and Facebook, both Trump and Bolsonaro work against the influence of mainstream media.

Bolsonaro is one of Brazil's "most influential politicians online," with more than 10.5 million followers on Twitter, Facebook and Instagram combined (Uchoa 2018). In Bolsonaro's media-led election campaign, Sérgio Costa observes the radical change of "political communication and thereby the foundations of democracy", which Bolsonaro plays to perfection (Costa 2018, translation JR). Other critics even speak of the construction of parallel worlds or realities, created through (social and other) media bubbles, and which lead to completely different patterns of perception (see e.g. Seeßlen 2017). One such pattern is the betrayal of the "general will" of "the people" through what is perceived as the "privileging" of minorities through affirmative action, gender and LGBTQI rights, and political correctness. During his visit to Trump in March 2019, Bolsonaro already hinted at one of his main policy targets: Brazil's affirmative action program, which had been enacted in 2001 to reduce inequalities based on racism, and later increasingly also on low-income status (which often coincides with racialization) (Roberts 2018). He thereby indicates that what is at stake is a struggle over cultural hegemony in a climate of diversified worldviews and lifestyles in the aftermath of 1968 and the consequent decreasing power of White male heteronormative orders. Costa observes structural parallels between Bolsonaro's campaign, the Brexit campaign in the UK, the campaigns by Donald Trump in the US and the *Alternative für Deutschland* (AfD) party in Germany with regard to several elements of this new communication pattern. These new forms of election campaigns are no longer about political arguments, but about the electorate's entire existence:

> In a parallel reality, the voters' entire way of life – as Christians, as nuclear families, as heterosexuals, as members of a nation – is being presented as severely threatened. The people – above all the male voters who become the center of such narratives – are stylized as heroes whose vote and everyday offensive stance can banish the threat. (Costa 2018, translation JR)

In order to create such a parallel reality, mainstream media that could put this parallel reality into question are usually disavowed – as the notorious "fake news" phenomenon indicates. Being in the defensive position, Costa argues, media often respond with positive coverage on their critics. However, following the populist logic, the presumed threat only becomes plausible when enemies are constructed that are threatening not a political position, but the existence of the community. In the current climate they make up for perceived threats caused by socio-economic insecurity. "These enemies are no abstract phenomena like globalization or global capitalism, but concrete opponents that can be recognized and fought on an everyday basis: 'illegal migrants' in the US or Britain, refugees and Muslims in Germany, and in Brazil: Gays or the sinful left" (Costa 2018, translation JR). Hence, the plurality of family models, free and legal abortion are constructed as a fundamental threat to the (reproduction/maintenance) of the nation. Costa argues that, in the course of the current transformation of political communication arguments, models of justice and concepts for a common future are replaced in politics by "emotions, disinformation, recipes for a 'good life' and solutions for presumably existential threats" (ibid.). The political establishment or elite and democratic institutions are also constructed as an enemy, since they are seen as incapable of protecting the people from these threats. And so are feminists, LGBTQI activists, and gender studies scholars, who are construed as threats to the family and the nation. As will be shown in the discussion of the following communicative patterns, the latter have recently been attacked by conservatives and right-wing populists under the heading of "gender ideology", a term originally coined by the Vatican to oppose emancipatory gender and sexual politics.

This tendency of right-wing deployment that we can also observe in the USA, in Germany or Britain has gained momentum in Brazil, particularly with regard to the importance of social media like WhatsApp as communicative tools and what Costa terms the "central role of religion and sexuality in the political discourse" (ibid.). During Bolsonaro's election campaign, WhatsApp played a pivotal role: Brazil has approx. 147 million voters and 120 million WhatsApp users, the latter of which do not all have regular access to the internet (see Gardels 2018). This is due to the fact that several mobile phone providers enable their clients the access to WhatsApp without extra costs, while navigating the Internet is complicated and expensive. WhatsApp thus advanced to become the most important electoral battlefield besides television, and Bolsonaro and his team knew how to use it for their cause and to their advantage. Over 80% of Bolsonaro's supporters received their information via WhatsApp (Datafolha institute, cf. in Costa 2018), which unlike other platforms such as YouTube or Facebook cannot be monitored by electoral authorities. After he became the victim of a knife attack on September 16, 2019, social media further helped Bolsonaro to stylize himself as a hero or savior and at the same time as normal citizen, as images of him from a hospital bed circulated broadly on YouTube and WhatsApp, and he also gave television interviews. He thus projected a personalized and private image that addressed people's feelings, while his opponents were fighting each other in television debates.

In the case of Donald Trump, media also have played a pivotal role for the success of his election campaign and for further mobilizing his followers. The role of Fox News as a private TV station supporting Trump is well-known, and so is the role of Breitbart News and Steve Bannon – who was one of the most important advisers for Trump in his election campaign and under his presidency, until he was fired in 2017. Bannon is also said to have advised Bolsonaro for his campaign as well as the German right-wing populist AfD party (Assheuer 2018). As a media professional who hosted a reality show ("The Apprentice") for 12 years, Trump knows how to deal with the logic of mass media and use them for his own purposes. Trump has a long experience of promoting himself as a success story, which is also evident in his books, which became bestsellers under telling titles such as *The Art of the Deal* (1987), *Think Big* (2007), *Never Give Up* (2008), or *Great Again: How to fix Our Crippled America* (2015). Through his strategic use of Twitter, Trump further makes use of the possibilities of new social media to seemingly communicate personally with and directly influence his followers as well as public discourse more generally. Trump usually sends his first Tweets early in the morning, before the first news of the day, and thereby sets the tone for particular topics. His consistent demonization of "traditional" and "serious" media, whom he accuses of producing "fake news", has further fed this logic and contributed to a deeply divided discourse of media and its role in democracy.

Since he cannot control the media like other populist leaders, Trump thus creates his own reality and his own discourse in opposition to all media that see him critically. Following the populist logic, Trump seems to be successful among his followers at undermining the authority of mainstream media as part of the "corrupt elite" that is "betraying the people" (Mitchell et al. 2017). He makes use of this logic by calling the media "the enemy of the people", questioning the reliability of the referee entirely. In a recent CBS News poll, 91% of Trump's "strong supporters" said they trust him to provide them with accurate information. Only 11% said the same thing about the "mainstream media" (see Zurcher 2018). The increasing role of affective ties further points to a changing notion of (what counts as) "truth" as opposed to "facts", particularly in a context where undesirable information is easily dismissed. A further important aspect is the content flows between social media and mainstream media supporting right-wing populist discourse. One interesting example is the daily morning program "Fox and Friends" which acts as a mouthpiece for Trump's tweets.

One pattern that can increasingly be found in right-wing populist discourse is the refusal to acknowledge historical wrongs, as is evident in Trump's racist remarks and Bolsonaro's disrespectful comments on slavery: "What debt of slavery? I never enslaved anyone in my life. Look, if you really look at history, the Portuguese didn't even step foot in Africa. The Blacks themselves turned over the slaves," he said in a TV interview in July 2018 (Roberts 2018). AfD politicians like Alexander Gauland in Germany have made similar arguments regarding the Holocaust, downplaying it as a speck of "bird shit" in history. Trump's comment that "both sides" were to blame for the escalations between promoters and opponents of the removal of civil war Confederate statues in Charlottesville goes in a similar direction. The effect is to cause controversy by saying publicly what many – the "silent majority", or the real "people" – are supposedly thinking and doing away with a shameful history by normalizing it through repetition, for which media play a crucial role. And since affect is one of the major currencies through which mass and particularly social media gain attention (showing emotions, dramatization, breaking taboos, causing scandals), gender plays a pivotal role as an arena within media discourses, and further as an "affective bridge" (Dietze 2019) as the examples in the following patterns show.

Media – and social media in particular – play a central role today for all populists, which is also due to the similar logics in the attention economy. Media have historically been crucial for the success of populist actors, as the example of the central role of radio for *Peronismo* shows. New social media furthermore provide the space for radical right-wing, mostly male extremists, Alt-right supporters (Strick 2019), for female supporters of right-wing populism like the Women for Trump, but also for the organization of resistance for social movements and anti-sexist campaigns. New media have both expanded and undercut the traditional roles of the press in a democratic society. New media have on the one hand vastly increased the potential for political information to reach even the most disinterested citizens and enable the creation of digital public spheres where opinions can be openly shared, creating new avenues for engagement that allow the public to connect with governments, and to contribute to the flow of political information (see Owen 2018). At the same time, however, "the coalescence of the rise of new media and post-truth society has made for a precarious situation that subverts their beneficial aspects" (ibid.). Indeed, it seems as if there are hardly any effective checks on the rising tide of false information. The replacement of serious investigative journalism by scandal coverage has weakened the media's democratic role: "The ambiguous position of the media as a mouthpiece for politicians renders journalists complicit in the proliferation of bad information and faulty facts" (ibid.). Diana Owen sees the current era as marking "a new low for the democratic imperative of a free press" (ibid.) Simon Tisdall (2018) even speaks of the "war" Donald Trump is fighting with the media as one with "deadly implications", whereas Costa (2018) and Seeßlen (2017) ascribe to social media, in combination with current forms of right-wing populism, the capacity to create "communicative bubbles" and "parallel realities". When all established authorities are called liars, the populist voice appears truthful in the sense of "honest" or "sticking to one's principles" which Brum defines as a "self-truth":

> Explaining hasn't had any effect. Bolsonaro is less a post-truth phenomenon than a phenomenon of what I call self-truth. The content of what he says doesn't matter: what matters is the act of saying it. Aesthetics have replaced ethics. By saying everything and anything, no matter how violent, he is labelled truthful or sincere by his voters at a time when politicians are being shunned as frauds and liars. At

> the same time, "truth" has become an absolute and a personal choice. The individual has been taken to a radical extreme. (Brum 2018)

As the instances of Trump's and Bolsonaro's openly sexist and misogynist remarks show, this "self-truth" seems to imply sticking to particular versions of hegemonic masculinity. Among their supporters, these versions seem to strengthen rather than threaten their popularity.

3.2. Pattern II: Appropriating Women's Politics for Femonationalist Arrangements

The "moral panic" (Rubin 1984, cf. Cohen 1981) caused by the perceived menace to the survival of the "nation"/ "people" justifies the cry for a "strong" (male) leader to re-install the (traditionally gendered) order against the decadent and menacing outcomes of the sexual revolution of the 1960s and 1970s and the related equality politics. Conservative churches and populist leaders both represent the patriarchal order, which they promise to maintain, defend, or, as the case may be, re-establish. Through the defense of a particular, hegemonic, masculinism – broadly understood as the ideology of patriarchy which seeks to value and include only male views – they transfer the political hierarchy to the gender hierarchy. Both the Trump and the Bolsonaro presidency follow the progressive, pluralist governments by Lula da Silva and Barack Obama. The former was the first representative of the working-class (and opponent to the military dictatorship) to hold the highest office, while the latter was the first African American man to do so. They also succeed the (relative) success of the first female presidential candidates, against whom both launched harsh struggles during their campaigns: Dilma Rousseff, who ran Brazil from 2011 to (her impeachment in) 2016 and Hillary Clinton, the first woman to run for US president. While Dilma Rousseff represents opposition to the military dictatorship during which she was imprisoned, Hillary Clinton counts as the prototypical US American (White middle-class) feminist. Gender played a decisive role in both campaigns, since it was through the condemnation of the female candidates' femininity and the ridiculing of these left-wing predecessors "weak", feminized – and in Obama's case racialized – masculinity that the candidates positioned themselves. When political differences and racial and class hierarchies are transferred to the gender hierarchy, the binary becomes legible and affectively accessible in terms of the gender binary.

Joseph Jay Sosa examines the sexism against Dilma Rousseff and the social imaginary of Brazil's rightward turn that he observes starting with Rousseff's rise to power. Analyzing three archetypes by which Rousseff was caricatured, a "subversive" (as a participant in the underground resistance to Brazil's military dictatorship), a "mother" ("caring" to the nation through welfare programs) and a "killjoy" (through her insistence on the rule of law), Sosa argues that "sexism catalyzed deep conservative cosmologies that allowed a cultural space for Brazil's rightward turn" (Sosa 2019, 717). As the first female president and also the first to lead a PT (workers' party) lead government into a second term, Rousseff continued the social welfare program *Bolsa Familia*, which led millions of poor and non-White Brazilian families out of poverty and had a decisive impact on Brazil's economic expansion in the early 2000s. Rousseff had to significantly change the policies she defined as family politics, however. The debates about abortion "rearticulated the ideological divide over gender and sexuality in Brazilian politics, with Brazil's first woman president as its increasingly reluctant arbiter" (730). While the conservative opposition delegitimized PT politicians as corrupt, arguing that they used social welfare programs to buy poor people's votes, they increasingly attacked Rousseff's bureaucratic performance as a "killjoy", as unable to be happy and thereby spoiling the happiness of others: "When the killjoy points out a problem to others, people begin to treat her as the problem" (736, cf. Ahmed 2010). Sosa concludes that the sexism against Rousseff provided a framework for projecting "conservative imaginaries of corruption, subversion, and family values" onto Rousseff and thereby draw away attention from questions of popular sovereignty and the rule of law. Sexism further served to communicate that Rousseff and her supporters "didn't belong to the nation" (723). During her presidency, the legalization of abortion and same-sex marriage caused heated debates, particularly among evangelical Christian actors who gained political influence, leading to "long-standing definitions of human rights and the family (…) being renegotiated" (727). Gender in this case served to unite right-wing populist and conservative religious voices in opposition to Rousseff's administration.

Misogynist descriptions, and thus "gender", not only served to disparage Rousseff, but it also formed the "cognitive and affective glue between accusations" (724). Similar gendered strategies were used by the right against presidential candidate Hillary Clinton in the 2016 election campaign, during which Trump and his supporters focused much of his campaign on delegitimizing and criminalizing Hillary Clinton, who would have been the first female president of the US. In both cases, the openly misogynist hatred for the oppositional women politicians who were cast as members of the ruling elite, the right-wing populist candidates represented the return of the "until then overshadowed" (Prandini Assis and Ogando 2018) strong patriarchal White leader. However, this ideology can no longer afford to exclude women. Rather, current right-wing populist discourse relies on the solidarity and support of particular women.

From an intersectional gender perspective, the role of Donald Trump's wife Melania and his daughter Ivanka are of particular interest. Trump's marriage to Melania represents the "sexual economy of the sugar daddy" (Seeßlen 2017, 37, translation JR), which supports his "leader" image. This type of women sanctifies the populist leader's power and appeal. Moreover, in the case of Melania and Ivanka Trump, these women are positioned as role models of attractiveness and wealth. Furthermore, Seeßlen (2017) observes a counter-narrative to the liberal gender and family order Obama had embodied to perfection, in which marriage is an equal partnership, and in which many voters might see their life style ridiculed, if not threatened. Seeßlen (2017) claims that many supporters approve of the gender arrangement represented by Trump: "in the sexual economy of this counter-narrative, the status of woman as luxury good is accepted" (43) – particularly if she demands a high prize. And he concludes that: "the Trump woman has an important function in the re-ordering of power, not despite but because of her Barbie and luxury goods existence" (47).

The figure of the Trump woman supports a new reality in which masculinism is accepted as "natural" male behavior, excusable as long as "he" stands by his wife and secures her lifestyle. Part of such a revival of traditional roles might be caused by the mentioned thus-perceived "emancipation fatigue". Not coincidentally, it was Melania Trump who poured oil on troubled water after her husband's "grab them by the pussy" video went viral by calling his sexist comments "locker room" talk (Gajanan 2016). Trivializing Trump's violent comments as tolerable "boys will be boys" behavior, Melania Trump catered to the electorates' desire to do away with the feminist political correctness that Hillary Clinton represented and that, in their view, forced men to "act against their nature" and question the traditional gender roles they considered natural and legitimate. Following the logic and "reality" of his electorate, Trump's "possession" of beautiful women burnishes his image as a self-made man. And vice versa, the women loyal to the populist leaders also gain by being awarded material wealth and positions of power. Trump's daughter Ivanka represents a strong, independent neoliberal feminist type. She helps Trump to attenuate and cushion his scandals, as we could see in her reaction to the Trump tapes, which she condemned as "unacceptable" while continuing to back her father, claiming to "know him" (Worley 2017). However, the fact that Trump seemingly "needs" Ivanka – who has taken on the role of de facto first lady – in order to make his masculinist sexist stance palatable to his female and conservative voters indicates that the workings of gender as an epistemic field within right-wing discourse must be read as a more complex pattern than as a simple backlash.

In strong contrast to the politics of diversity promoted by Lula, Dilma, Obama, and Hillary Clinton, Trump and Bolsonaro – in different ways and to different extents – cater to or support the conservative Christian and right-wing populist notion of the nuclear, heterosexual family as the nucleus of the state to which "gender ideology" stands in stark opposition. All of these predecessors represent key "enemies" within right-wing populist discourse: following this perspective they stand for the "(left/East Coast) elite", left-wing danger, "political correctness" – and "gender ideology". The election campaigns of both candidates demonstrate how the depiction of their predecessors (and, in Clinton's case, competitors) served as perfect projections for representing everything that he himself would not do and not stand for. "The message from these forces was clear: women and LGBTQI people were and are not welcome in politics, and more powerfully: gender and sexual justice ideals and agendas are even less so" (Prandini Assis and Ogando 2018). For Mariana Prandini Assis and Ana Carolina Ogando (2018), then, the "crusade" against "gender ideology" in Bolsonaro's presidential campaign reinforced a hegemonic, masculine and violent form of not only 'doing politics' but even inhabiting the world" (ibid.). This confrontational style of politics has already started to result in the "annihilation" of its chosen enemies from the public sphere and the rapidly increasing number of violent acts against women and differently gendered and non-white bodies in Brazil and the US (ibid.).

In Trump's rhetoric, we see the right-wing populist logic of "pro women, against feminists", (cf. Gutsche 2018) as he defends the "freedom" of ("autochthonous"/ "our") American women, while repeatedly stating that he supports traditional marriage (that is, against gay marriage and other family models). However, the fact that Trump did not – at least not publicly – condemn feminists, but rather refused to be identified as one, shows that he is well aware that he needs to react to certain emancipatory ideas and at least create these paradoxes and distract attention from a clear line of his gender and sexual politics. His mode, however, relies on the appropriation of femininity for (re)enforcing masculinity and patriarchy while "selling" it as happening with the consent of women as some sort of emancipatory politics (in the sense of his daughter Ivanka's feminism).

A recent study by the German Friedrich Ebert Foundation (FES) titled *Triumph of the Women? The Female Face of the Populist & Far Right in Europe* (Gutsche 2018) demonstrates how right-wing populist parties present themselves as defenders of women's rights (particularly White women) and simultaneously advocate anti-emancipatory positions. The comparative study of the "female face" in six European countries shows that while men still dominate in most populist parties, the number of women is increasing, and women are becoming more and more prominent in leadership positions of right-wing populist parties. These parties seek to limit immigration and emphasize a distinct cultural identity. Sauer (Sauer 2017, cf. Lang 2015) sees the challenge for rightwing actors today exactly in the new position of women in right-wing groups and parties and in their openly expressed leadership claim, as right-wing women, who used to be responsible for the maintenance of the group, are now oriented as well to the interior/private and the exterior/political and can thereby be won over as followers, voters, or officials. Often, these women are among the strongest supporters of anti-feminist and anti-genderist politics. As the FES study also shows, the number of women voting for right-wing populist parties is increasing, while still being much smaller than that of the male voters. This tendency could also be observed during the election campaigns in the US and Brazil, where women formed a considerable part of the electorate – despite the candidates' outright sexist and misogynist remarks. And in both contexts, we also saw groups of women publicly speaking out and campaigning for the candidates, such as the "Women for Trump" (Morrison 2018) in the US or the *Mulheres com Jair Bolsonaro Presidente* (Women with President Jair Bolsonaro) in Brazil (Kaiser 2018). A common argument among these groups is that gender equality already exists – and the different roles taken are the result of individual choices and values – and that feminism discriminates against men (and is thus "anti-male" and "anti-equality") (Watson 2018; see also Prandini Assis and Ogando 2018). Trump's White House counselor Kellyanne Conway repeatedly underscored her critique of feminism, which she stigmatized as anti-male and pro-abortion:

> It's difficult for me to call myself a feminist in the classic sense because it seems to be very anti-male and it certainly is very pro-abortion, and I'm neither anti-male or pro-abortion. So, there's an individual feminism, if you will, that you make your own choices (…). I look at myself as a product of my choices, not a victim of my circumstances. (Conway, cf. in Scott 2018)

Conway thus also promotes her version of "common sense" based on neoliberal incorporations of feminist ideas, seeing her own achievements as a result of individual decisions, not the underlying power structures that create inequalities from which she benefits. In a binary manner, feminism is consequently constructed as "anti-male" and "pro-abortion". Similar arguments were already found among the representatives of the Tea Party movement such as Sarah Palin, who saw their way of life menaced by the liberal feminism represented by Hillary Clinton. Notably, Donald Trump has also stated that he is "not a feminist", because "he is for everyone": "I'm for women, I'm for men, I'm for everyone" (Scott 2018; Cohen 2017). As Trump's comments indicate, right-wing populists tend to reduce feminism to an ideology that promotes the hatred of men, which fits neatly into their Manichean worldview. His comments also oppose Barack Obama's politics of diversity, as expressed in a speech at the 2016 United States Women's Summit in Washington D.C., in which Obama presented himself with the words "I may be a little grayer than I was eight years ago, but this is what a feminist looks like" (Rhodan 2016).

This phenomenon can also be observed in the important role of right-wing "token women", who appear either as supporters of right-wing candidates or parties, or as politicians in their own right. Significantly, Bolsonaro abolished the human rights ministry in favor of a newly created "ministry of women, family, human rights and indigenous people", for which he chose the (female) evangelical pastor and severe anti-feminist Damares Alves as minister of family affairs. Under the left-wing president Dilma Rousseff, Brazil had a Ministry of Women, Racial Equality and Human Rights, which her successor Michel Temer downgraded into a Secretariat for Women's Policies, first under the Justice Ministry, then, in June 2018 under the Human Rights Ministry (Phillips 2018). The new ministry will also be in charge of the National Foundation of the Indigenous (FUNAI), a previously independent institution that regulates issues related to the indigenous communities in the country. FUNAI is in charge of protecting the areas inhabited by indigenous groups and is one of Brazil's last lines of defense against extractivist projects in the territory. Tying it to the ministry will put it at the hands of Alves and Bolsonaro, who are against reservations because of the limitations to private companies' interests (Telesur 2018). Alves, who is decidedly "Pro-life" and has been quoted saying "we want a Brazil without abortion" and has emphasized that "women are born to be mothers" (Phillips 2018) has been met with concern by indigenous representatives and feminists. Like Trump's White House advisor Conway, Alves sees feminism in an interview in March 2018 as anti-male: "It's as if there was a war between men and women in Brazil. This does not exist" (Phillips 2018). Interestingly, Alves defended same-sex marriage, which is legal in Brazil, and declared her support for LGBTI movements (Phillips 2018, Telesur 2018).

However, she is also against sexual education in schools, reflecting Bolsonaro's will to scrap sexual education from public schools' curricula and forbid the use of concepts such as "gender perspective". Alves' conservative and populist position is also expressed through the fact that she is one of the founders of *Atini – Voz Pela Vida* (Voice for Life), a group dedicated to adopting and relocating indigenous children from communities and educating them in evangelical Christianity; Alves has herself adopted an indigenous girl. She also represents an exemplary case for the trend of anti-feminism as an alliance for the "good" of the "people" or nation. Anti-genderism thus functions as a sort of remedy for containing gender hierarchies and male privilege, a structure that replaces and expands anti-feminism against gender studies as an alternative model of knowledge (Dietze 2015, 126, cf. Maihofer and Schutzbach 2015).

Religiously motivated conservative women like Alves identify with naturalized traditional gender roles, justifying their support with their interest in the well-being and protection of children, family, and the nation, as well as "Pro-life" politics. They gain power by aligning themselves with men through racism (in the same way that women are important for male populists, racialized others are important for right-wing women). As Seeßlen (2017, 43) argues, besides the traditional, reactionary gender roles Trump represents, many of his female voters may have voted for him despite his sexism, because they consider his other promises, such as the wall against aliens, the economic "salvation" and the reconstruction of a lost greatness and order, as more important. By demonizing feminism as "anti-male", "sexist", and exclusive, the Women for Trump and Women for Bolsonaro movements further represent a form of Occidentalist self-assurance via a better gender regime, a notion which enables the participant women to see themselves as fully emancipated and not affected by structural discrimination – which is projected onto other women and "cultures", while White women "gain" an advantage through their femonationalist alliance with White men against immigrants (see Farris 2012 and 2017). By distinguishing itself from non-heteronormative and non-binary sexualities and other "enemies" such as feminists and "gender ideology", the Occidentalist superiority is further constructed, defined and maintained. Gendered discourses thus help bring together a broad alliance of conservative voices. The opposition to emancipatory gender politics – or against "gender ideology" – politically and ideologically selectively unites these actors. Family and gender policies are one of the key areas in this domain.

3.3. Pattern III: (White) Re-Masculinization: "Genderism" as Existential Threat

During his reunion with Donald Trump in March 2019, Jair Bolsonaro claimed to stand on common ground with Trump in their shared rigid opposition to "the gender ideology".

The Obama administration had implemented several federal programs that broadened the legal concept of gender as an individual choice and not assigned at birth or predetermined by biology. Trump, prodded by conservatives and evangelical Christians, aims at establishing a legal definition of (biological) sex under Title IX, the government funded federal civil rights law that bans gender discrimination in education programs (Green, Benner and Pear 2018). The Trump administration has sought to stop transgender people from serving in the army and has legally challenged civil rights protections for trans individuals embedded in the nation's health care law, insisting on defining gender as strictly biologically determined (Green, Benner and Pear 2018). Several agencies have withdrawn policies that recognized gender identity in schools, prisons and homeless shelters, and the Trump administration even tried to delete questions about gender identity from a 2020 census survey and a national survey of elderly citizens and to remove 'gender' from UN human rights documents (Borger 2018). In doing so, Trump was catering to the demands of conservative Christian actors like Roger Severino, former director of the DeVos Center for Religion and Civil Society at the Heritage Foundation, who was among the conservatives who felt intimidated by the Obama administration's expansion of sex to include gender identity, which he called "radical gender ideology".

While Trump is a newcomer to politics – and represents a sort of "outsider" perspective, since he does not identify with the Republican Party line – Bolsonaro looks back on a long career in politics, during which he already promoted positions he can now push with more force. As a congressman for 28 years, he frequently made disparaging comments about gays, women, indigenous groups and

Blacks. While such comments always draw sharp criticism, they also garner him attention and feed his narrative of being somebody unencumbered by political correctness. Bolsonaro was among the first opponents to the 2011 Supreme Court decision that legalized the recognition of same-sex couples. He was supported in this by the evangelical parliamentary block that was also crucial for his successful presidential candidacy, which seeks to undermine the expansion of sexual and reproductive rights, same sex marriage and the right to legal, free and safe abortion. Also, in 2011, Bolsonaro led a campaign against inclusionary educational materials developed by the Ministry of Education, which were to challenge the discrimination and violence against LGBTQI groups. Demonizing them as a "gay kit", Bolsonaro castigated the program as a menace to the sexual binary and to Brazilian children and families; the materials were subsequently abandoned by the Ministry. And yet, when confronted by journalists with a video showing two gay men having sex in public he had posted during the carnival when he visited the US, Bolsonaro also denied being a homophobe. The Trump administration in the USA and several European governments have recently developed a similar rhetoric, as can be observed with the AfD in Germany, Victor Orbán's anti-gender crusade in Hungary or similar movements in Poland, Spain, or Austria. Analogue narratives had been circulated already since the 1990s in conservative Catholic and conservative intellectual circles (see Case 2019).

Sabine Hark and Paula Irene Villa (2015) define "anti-genderism" as an "'anti'-stance, a rejection against gender" as a non-natural and thereby post-essentialist form of gender (and sexuality) (7). Further, they present the accusations of those they call the "anti-gender alliance", whose terminology "pseudo-science", or "gender craze" (ibid. 18, translations JR). openly and vehemently attack researchers dedicated to the topic. In the right-wing devaluation of an entire research area, the authors see a "deeply anti-democratic attack on the freedom of research and teaching" (Hark and Villa 2015, 33, translation JR). A related "war on gender ideology" (Prandini Assis and Ogando 2018) is also expressed in new waves of sexist, racist, homophobic and transphobic violence for which the assassination of the Brazilian openly gay Black politician Marielle Franco stands symbolically. Achievements that had been taken for granted by many are again being challenged; numerous right-wing populist parties make racist and sexist language socially acceptable, and the Bolsonaro government has continued the rapid reduction of affirmative action politics and institutions that president Lula da Silva had introduced.

Trump has taken a critical stance on gay marriage, but he declared that the decision should remain with individual states. After the Supreme Court's decision on the legality of homosexual marriage, he declared that this decision needed to be accepted and would no longer serve as an election campaign topic. In September 2015, he even asked the civilian administrator Kim Davis from Kentucky to stop refusing marriage certificates for homosexual couples. Other Republicans have criticized Trump for his liberal position in this regard. Trump thus seemingly has an ambiguous position and no clear religious agenda or doctrine, but rather uses different arguments for different strategies he pursues, or consciously keeps in a state of ambiguity.

In his 2000 book *The America We Deserve*, Trump expressed his pro-choice position in relation to abortion, and he later emphasized his stance in an interview. Only during the 2016 presidential campaign did he declare to be "Pro-life" and thus against abortions, presumably in order to gain acceptance and support among conservative Republicans. However, Trump has also said he is for the right to abortion in certain cases. This inconsistent position points to his strategic employment of gender topics, which Trump uses and interprets to serve his political aims, not out of political or moral conviction.

As the complex constellations and alliances in these examples have shown, more seems to be at stake than a mere revolt by the socially marginalized. More complex, intersectional and varying dynamics are at play, in which a (perceived) precarious state is mixed with and/or crisscrossed by a variety of factors such as fear of loss of privilege and the desire for the maintenance – or gain – of supremacy. Weronika Grzebalska, Eszter Kováts and Andrea Petö (2018) emphasize the affective effects of right-wing populist politics and argue that the concept of "gender ideology" has become a metaphor for the unequal socioeconomic order, a signifier of the perceived failure of democratic representation, and a means of rejecting "different facets" of this order. Equality politics have come to signify "everything that is wrong with the current state of politics" (33), ranging from the perceived prioritization of identity politics over social and material issues, and the climate of social, cultural and political security, to the alienation of social and political elites and the growing influence of transnational institutions and the global economy (34). The authors argue that besides demonizing political correctness and the human rights paradigm, the opposition to "gender ideology" is mobilized by offering an alternative that centers on nation, family, religious values and freedom of speech, and "rests on a positive identification of an individual's own choice, and one that promises a safe and secure community as a remedy to individualism and atomization" (34). Finally, through the opposition to gender politics and left-wing agendas (identity politics) – which reconnects with long-standing historic exclusionary ideologies – right-wing populists have managed to unite and create alliances among a number of actors, including religious groups ranging from Christian churches, fundamentalist Muslims and Jews to far right parties and conservatives (34). Social media play a key role in forming "bubbles" and "networks" or "communities" of similar minded people, as well as emphasizing the scapegoat function of anti-genderism.

The right-wing politics of anti-genderism and anti-Affirmative Action programs cater to the right-wing populist notion of a menace to the family and the nation. Affirmative action programs and gender rights activists are imagined as unjustly advantaging minorities, who enjoy privileges that are denied to the "real" people. Through the idea of a globally spread menace of "gender ideology", this threat is projected onto the global scale and given a religious dimension, and as a fundamental and all-encompassing menace.

3.4. Pattern IV: Reverse Anti-Colonialism: "Gender Ideology" as "Ideological Colonization", Radical Religious and Femoglobal Alliances

Photo no. 4: Demo for everyone. 4,300 people demonstrated on 28 February 2016 in Stuttgart for marriage and family and against gender ideology and sexualization of children. February 2016. Flickr.

While the Trump administration has taken a clear stance against certain notions and policies of gender, Prandini Assis and Ogando emphasize the connections between Jair Bolsonaro's openly violent tone against women and LGBTQI communities in Brazil and what they describe as a globally growing movement promoting "the cultural-religious war on so-called 'gender ideology'." (Prandini Assis and Ogando 2018, cf. Case 2019) The term "gender ideology" originated with the Vatican in the 1990s, when a strategy that came to be known as gender mainstreaming – progressive efforts to make gender equality a central focus of UN documents and policies – entered politics.

In both of our exemplary cases of the United States and Brazil, the governments count on the broad support of the Catholic church and parts of the more fundamentalist Evangelical and Pentecostal churches. Donald Trump himself belongs to the Presbyterian Church, but is not religious. In his lifestyle, choice of words and the number of his marriages, Trump represents no Church-bound ideal. In fact, he is considered the "most profane" president of the US and the only one who got into office not because of his religiousness, but despite its absence (Süddeutsche Zeitung 2017). However, Trump builds on a circle of evangelical advisors he founded during his election campaign, consisting predominantly of pastors of mega churches. His spiritual advisor is TV pastor Paula White, who is a representative of Pentecostal theology and a philosophy of "positive thinking" and the "prosperity gospel" (Bassimir 2018, 392). While Trump is supported by numerous evangelical actors, this partnership seems to be predominantly a strategic one, garnering him both votes and support.

Jair Bolsonaro, in contrast to Donald Trump, has always been a devoted believer. Although baptized as a Roman Catholic, he has been attending services of the Baptist Church to which his wife and children belong since 2008. His third marriage – a not-so-pious life circumstance he shares with Trump – was held in the Pentecostal church *Assambleia de Deus*, and in 2016, he even was baptized for a second time in the river Jordan by pastor of the Pentecostal Church *Assambleia de Deus* and leader of the *Partido Social Cristão* Everaldo Pereira. Bolsonaro's social and political views are close to the Pentecostal positions, and he is strongly supported by the church.

Mary Ann Case (2019) argues that the current anti-gender politics in the US, such as Trump's exclusion of trans persons from the army backed by Catholics, Evangelicals, and other conservative forces go back to a long trajectory of religious anti-gender discourses outside the US. Tracing the respective postures of Pope Benedict from Germany and Pope Francis from Argentina as well as related "broader intellectual currents", Case links the local expressions to a global circulation of these positions through the immense power and broad acceptance of the religious leaders. Notably, as Case argues, both popes deployed their anti-genderist discourse against the backdrop of particular pro-gender legislative decisions. During the 1994 Cairo International Conference on Population and Development, and the Preparatory and Committee Meetings for the IV World Conference on Women (Beijing 1995), the Vatican articulated harsh attacks against such measures, which reached a wider audience through publications by Catholic conservative groups based in the United States, such as "The Gender Agenda" by female Catholic pro-life journalist Dale O'Leary, and other Vatican documents that included references by Cardinal Joseph Ratzinger (later Pope Benedict) prior to his papacy. Without using the term "gender" yet, the Ratzinger Report of 1980 had already put together all of the elements of what conservative opponents would come to call the "ideology of gender" (see Case 2019, 640). This happened in a context in which both public discourse and the legal climate in Germany opened up in a more emancipatory direction. German federal legislation legalized sex change procedures for trans persons, while feminist publications highlighting the social construction of gender roles became bestsellers. Ratzinger brought a strongly conservative anti-genderist stance to the Vatican. For the Vatican, the term gender would serve to deconstruct sex differences and lead to the dismantling of traditional family values, fostering "a war between the sexes, the devaluation of motherhood, the promotion of contraception and abortion, the acceptance of homosexual partnerships and parentage, and the decline of marriage" (Prandini Assis and Ogando 2018). When Francis took office in Rome as pope, his home country Argentina had implemented one of the world's "most generous" laws on transgender rights as well as several other emancipatory measures in the realm of gender equality, such as the legalization of same-sex marriage and paid surrogacy (2010) and other forms of artificial procreation (2011).

Pope Francis appears to be less rigid concerning gender issues than his German predecessor. However, soon after entering office, Francis introduced the notion of "ideological colonization" to condemn governments and NGOs from the EU and the US or other multinational or supranational institutions that tie grants for the education of the poor "to the condition that 'gender theory' [be] taught" (Francis 2015, cf. in Case 2019, 649). In this statement, by speaking for "the poor" and simultaneously envisioning "their" values – which seemingly coincide with those of the Catholic church – to be corrupted and menaced by "gender ideology", Francis reverses the gaze and hierarchy of classical victim discourse. This discourse is also found in left wing and activist critiques of Western development policies. Together with the "poor" victims of such measures, conservative Catholic gender hierarchies can thus be portrayed as forming part of a minority under attack. It is not the church that is proselytizing "the poor", but, in Francis' rhetorical twist, all Catholics – and other conservative Christians and believers of other faiths – can imagine themselves as victims whose values and identities are severely threatened. A similar pattern can also be observed among (predominantly but not exclusively White male) internet activists around the so-called Alt-Right, who see "genderism" as an oppressive regime and themselves not as aggressors, but in a condition of permanent threat (see e.g. Diehl et al. in Der Spiegel 2019 tracing the connections of Christchurch attacker Brenton Tarrant with right-wing networks).

Pope Francis has expressed his harshest opposition to educational materials on sexual diversity. It is ideologies such as this that make it into broad sectors of societies and can be found across the political and social spectrum and in many locations. Through this position, Francis has gained approval far beyond the traditional conservatives, finding "resonance with the allegedly colonized, from the global South to Eastern Europe." (Case 2019, 650) And, as Case claims, his position resonates particularly in the US. The term and concept of "gender ideology" or a "gender agenda" has only recently been adopted by right-wing "US Catholic culture warriors." It serves them the useful function of addressing a number of aspects under one umbrella term. As Case observes, "a disproportionate number" of public pronouncements, such as those by military chaplain Timothy Broglio, address topics on what the Vatican demonizes as the "gender agenda". Case concludes that feminist and trans rights claims are "not a recent addition, but rather a foundational component, (...) to the Vatican's sphere of concern around 'gender' and to the focusing of that concern on developments in secular law." (Case 2019, 640) Gender thus seems to serve a particular function within the Vatican's discourses as well as in the context of the increasing alliances between conservative Catholic actors, right-wing populist protagonists, and radical right-wing movements. The right-wing Catholic-inspired discourse offers such actors political representation, affirms their traditional views and ways of life, and defends them against the challenges they perceive. Case references the Humanum conference, an international colloquium hosted at the Vatican in 2014 dedicated to "the complementarity of man and woman" and the importance of marriage. This conference included people from many different faiths, including many of the United States' anti-LGBTI conservatives. The conference provides a showcase example for the unifying character of gender – or, rather, anti-genderism or the fight against "gender ideology" – as a common ground on which to address their concerns and attack the common enemy:

> The 2014 Humanum conference offers the public face of this future: with US money, it brought to the very heart of the Vatican representatives of faith traditions whose principal point of commonality with the Vatican is their mutual opposition to LGBT, women's, and reproductive rights, (...) opposition to gender ideology has united conservative Catholics with persons of other faiths around the world with whom they agree on little other than the need to fight 'gender ideology'. (Case 2019, 658)

In Latin America, anti-gender campaigns have gained momentum against the backdrop of the rise of Pentecostal and Neo-Pentecostal religious groups and the simultaneous weakening of progressive – and partly female – presidencies in Argentina, Brazil and Chile. As Prandini Assis and Ogando point out, conservative religious groups joined forces with increasingly populist oppositional political elites in heated debates "to present 'gender ideology' as a common enemy" (Prandini Assis and Ogando 2018). Gender ideology thus has come to serve the function of an "enemy within" and simultaneously as an "outside" global threat. Thereby, gender plays a crucial role within the populist logics by constructing these enemies as a threat to the community and (the "natural" reproduction) of the nation. Gender can constantly be re-signified and create different enemies through the "moral panic" caused by sexual politics (ibid.) and as an existential menace.

Anticolonialism, or the anti-colonial frame envisioned by the right, provides a "new language" I call "Reverse Anti-Colonialism", in tune with populist logics that demonize global elites and defend the 'ordinary people' by equating gender egalitarianism with colonization. Religious conservatives, on the other hand, are presented as an embattled minority. The women aligning themselves with this notion expand a femonationalist frame to an international, femoglobal, scale. Their advantage is being able to imagine themselves as already fully emancipated and being in possession of the more advanced and morally superior sexual regime, from which defenders of other models and positions are excluded.

3.5. Pattern V: "Ethno-sexism" and "Exclusive Intersectionality" (Gendering of Social Inequalities and Gendering of Fear)

In her study of Tea Party supporters in Louisiana, *Strangers in Their Own Land*, sociologist Arlie Russell Hochschild (2016) examined the emotional make-up of people who feel outpaced by women and African Americans, who, in their eyes, receive undeserved support that is denied to those who have been waiting in line for much longer. As Hochschild elaborates, promises such as Trump's "Make America Great Again" slogan provide these supporters emotional relief and euphoria in the face of the menace of global capitalism whose victims they have become. Numerous theoreticians of current right-wing populism emphasize the function of this logic – a praxis of interpellation and communicative scheme of constructing inner enemies (gender studies approaches feminist and LGBQTI activists) as well as outer enemies (immigrants, a globally threatening "gender ideology") as a menace to their security, values and survival. Right-wing populism accordingly functions as a relief and a reactionary gesture in the complex world of (neo)liberalism, expressed in the hatred and construction of the threat of the liberal world. Following this pattern, right-wing populism works as an attack on the communicative forms of "liberal populism" (Stegemann 2017, 94) and its concrete representatives such as political, cultural and media elites or gays and feminists – or "gender ideology" – instead of the economic structures and social inequalities.

In her "Four Theses on the Relation between Right-Wing Populism and Anti-Genderism (and a Half on its Overcoming)", Eva von Redecker situates the function of racism and sexist ideologies in the context of capitalist modes of production as enabling the exploitation of the respective groups and for "sweetening" the life of the White male working class, who can feel symbolically superior despite their economically precarious situation. When the erosion of ideological hierarchies makes economic precarity virulent, as in the context of neoliberal intensification, right-wing populism manages to short-circuit experiences of precarity through the irritation of the symbolic loss of status and to deviate it through enemy images (von Redecker 2017). It is highly debatable however, whether this phenomenon can so easily be reduced to the "White working class", since supporters of right-wing populist ideas are constituted increasingly of bourgeois and middle-class men and women.

Trump's politics demonstrate very illustratively how negative external ascription serves to produce a sense of one's own superiority via the colonial pattern of "Occidentalism" – the construction of a superior Western self as condition of possiblity for constructing an inferior "Orientalist" Other (Coronil 1996) – and to distract from one's own emancipatory deficits (and misogyny and sexism), a discourse Dietze has defined in analogy to the posture of an "American exceptionalism" (positioning the US as the best and most "completed" version of all societies and democracies) as "sexual exceptionalism" (Dietze 2016). Representatives of the pro-

Trump or pro-Bolsonaro movements or figures like openly gay politician Alice Weidel of the AfD party in Germany represent to different extents the phenomenon of the exploitation and co-optation of feminist themes by anti-Islam and xenophobic campaigns that Sara R. Farris describes as "femonationalism" (Farris 2012 and 2017). By characterizing Muslim or non-White/non-"belonging" males as dangerous to Western societies and as oppressors of women, and by emphasizing the need to rescue Muslim and migrant women, these groups use gender equality to justify their racist rhetoric and policies. Similar arguments can also be found in the rhetoric of certain gay and LGBTQI groups who join a nationalist discourse with racist and xenophobic arguments and are often co-opted by right-wing groups, a phenomenon Jasbir Puar (2007) has referred to as "homonationalism". Farris analyzes how this practice also serves an economic function, as neoliberal civic integration policies and feminist groups include Muslim and non-Western immigrant women into the segregated domestic and care industries, all the while claiming to promote their emancipation. Through these inclusions, conversely, White women benefit through their coalition with White men. Thus, on the one hand, through the "ethno-sexist" (Dietze 2016b) narrative of the immigrant or Muslim sexual perpetrator, purportedly oppressed and silenced masculinities can imagine themselves once again as "protectors". For right-wing populists, the transgression of the naturalized gender and ethnic/cultural/national borders – which define binary, hierarchical gender positions and heterosexuality as the norm and 'natural' order – threatens the alleged homogeneity. The exclusion of the transgressor of this order/community and the suspension of marginalized groups such as immigrants is thereby justified, a strategic use of gender and ethnicity for processes of Othering dynamics or exclusive intersectionality that Sauer has referred to as "intersectionality from above" (Sauer 2013). Ironically, Gayatri Spivak's famous line about "White men saving Brown women from Brown men" is in this scenario shifted to a female (and, partly, feminist) alliance with nationalist-conservative and right-wing racist discourse that could be paraphrased as

"White women saving Brown women from Brown men" – while the male position sticks to an imaginary of "White men saving White women from Brown men." (See also Dietze 2013 who elaborates on the long tradition of this pattern in the US, embodied by the so-called rape-lynching complex.)

In most current right-wing populist discourses, the inability – or, rather, failure or reluctance – of liberal or left-wing politics to protect national borders from "illegal" and unwanted immigration is mobilized as a central trope and as a severe threat to the very existence of the "autochthonous" "culture" and population. Both Donald Trump and Jair Bolsonaro work toward strict immigration policies, through the policing and militarization of their national borders. They both also mobilize seemingly feminist (or pro-women) arguments to negotiate topics like demography, citizenship and belonging and immigration (defense). Right after his inauguration, Trump began to dismantle the DACA (Deferred Action for Childhood Arrivals) program for the temporary protection from deportation and the right to live, study and work in the USA for children of migrants granted under the Obama administration. He implemented his "Muslim ban" prohibiting visas for citizens of seven predominantly Muslim countries, and he promised to build a militarized wall between the US and Mexico to curb illegal immigration. Furthermore, Trump has continuously emphasized his aim to give up the current jus solis of US citizenship law. He has often argued that this law motivated Mexican migrant women to come to the US to have children in order to secure US citizenship, as expressed in the discourse on so-called "anchor babies" (see Boatcă and Roth 2016 and 2019). During his election campaign, he caused an outrage when he characterized Mexican immigrants as rapists – and thereby threatening the "autochthonous" women and the future of the "heartland/nation" – and as drug smugglers and criminals. When the parents of US Army Captain Humayun Khan, a Muslim soldier killed in the Iraq War, denounced Trump's comments on immigration and Islam at the Democratic National Convention, Trump attacked them and claimed that Khan's mother should have remained silent because her religion required it. Trump caused another media scandal when he defined Haiti, El Salvador and parts of Africa as "shithole countries" (Kendi 2019), language which implies a clear racial hierarchy. Ibram X. Kendi (2019) emphasizes that Trump places whites over Asians, and both over Latinos and blacks from "shithole" countries and concludes that Trump's "shithole countries" remark is evidence that he is more pro-white than anti-immigrant.

Like Trump, Bolsonaro has repeatedly rhetorically drawn a parallel between the nation and a family home, in phrases such as "our house (...) our Brazil" (Espinoza and Brumat 2018). Directly after his inauguration in January 2019, Bolsonaro withdrew from the UN pact on migration – which the Trump government had refused to sign to begin with (Paris 2019). He also implemented strict border regimes, particularly in the North of Brazil and currently at the border to Venezuela (see Espinoza and Brumat 2018). Tellingly, during his March 2019 visit to Trump, Bolsonaro promised to remove the visa "restrictions" for US citizens (which are/were actually reciprocal, since Brazil is/was the only country to introduce the same rules for obtaining visa for US citizens that the US requires from that country's own citizens).

Both leaders express a strongly White supremacist and anti-immigrant stance, but the related shifting alliances and narratives are at times contradictory. The correspondent paradox of "anti-genderism" is expressed through the fact that, while pursuing an outright anti-feminist aim, many right-wing populist actors simultaneously defend the liberty and emancipation of "their own" women, thereby performing a liberal, if not feminist, politics. Dietze describes such apparent contradictions in right-wing populist discourse as "dynamic paradoxes" in which the re-traditionalization program is merged with a supposed 'emancipation' program and brings together seemingly contradictory factors – programmatic gender conservatism, female leadership, and the claim that Western women are already emancipated. The paradox consists in the *simultaneity* of traditional core convictions and an "emancipation performance" (Dietze 2018, 36) in order to modernize right-wing gender models and uncouple them from radical right-wing stigma. These contradictions are not resolved, but are in motion and are being constantly re-negotiated (35). Such a "simulated progressiveness" (Dietze 2015) has the further effect of playing down one's own emancipation deficits and "silencing women's and gay activists through an "Occidental dividend", and co-opting them for an anti-immigration position. In a similar manner as in the so-called "New Year's Events" in Cologne, Germany, in 2015/16, Trump in his figure of the "Mexican rapist", projected the threat of sexual violence onto an outside enemy, immigrant, non-white men, from whom "women" had to be protected. Through this form of "ethno-sexism" (Dietze 2018), on the one hand, restrictions in immigration policies could be justified, and, on the other hand, the "proper" society could be imagined as free from sexual violence. Through such "outsourcing" of sexism/sexual violence accompanied by strategies of the described "intersectionality from above", right-wing populist actors can perform a strategy of modernization or even emancipation, while simultaneously maintaining their conservative positions. Right-wing populist communication strategies thus provide an important tool in the modernization of right-wing extremism. However, this modernization is geared more towards its public appeal than a change of the content or the ideological outlook.

4. Resume Part I: Orchestrating Contradictions Affectively

The first part of this study has investigated the ways in which gender is used in right-wing populist discourse as an epistemological scene, for the ordering and hierarchization of paradoxes and contradictions. The right-wing populist communicative patterns described above are part of a general struggle over cultural hegemony and social welfare/redistribution, in the context of globalized neoliberal capitalism in crisis. In right-wing debates, gender became an "empty signifier" and could thus be used in the struggle over cultural and political hegemony, in which right-wing populist actors oppose the liberal cultural tendencies and the perceived "social democratic" constellation for redistribution and integration (Sauer 2017, 15). New "masculinist" actors, such as bloggers of the Alt-Right et al., depict themselves as the victims of rigid feminists and gender studies ideologists who violently push through political correctness and threaten White male identity and the maintenance and "purity" of the nation at large. Through the demonization of gender studies and feminist approaches, these actors seek to naturalize differences and hierarchies. As a metaphor for naturalized hierarchies, gender serves the populist logic of polarization. Through the affective dimension usually attached to gender issues, gender also serves as an arena – or "affective bridge" (Dietze 2019) – for causing scandals that attract attention and distract from other issues, thus "channeling" other political and social discourses. Gender questions provide a useful field for the mobilization of affects through which a "politics of fear" can be orchestrated and distract attention from abstract menaces such as neoliberal capitalism (Sauer 2017).

The first pattern – *Gender as "Affective Bridge" in (Mass) Media* – has demonstrated the fundamental role of (mass) media for right-wing populist discourse. Proceeding from the observation that populism and mass media share a variety of similar logics and systemic affinities, mass media – and, increasingly, social media – play a crucial role for current right-wing populist actors, including the creation of echo chambers or "bubbles", breaking taboos, causing scandals and affective responses. Since (particularly commercial) media depend on large audiences, populist actors help them gain viewers through their continuous disregard for taboo, the production of scandal and the affective appeal and simplicity of their arguments. On the other hand, mass media and social media help populist actors to catapult their simple and affectively loaded arguments into the public sphere and, in the case of social media, to their carefully selected target groups and potential supporters. As the examples from Brazil and the US and the different communicative patterns typical for current right-wing discourse have demonstrated, gender is being used as suitable "meta language" in order to talk about demography, ethnicity, occidental entitlement, transfer payments, and anti-immigration. Gender – expressed in paradoxical patterns ranging from sexist and misogynist "locker room talk" to "anti-genderism" and "sexual exceptionalism" – is increasingly interpolated by numerous right-wing populist actors in order to affectively bridge these contradictions.

The second pattern, *Appropriating Women's Politics for Femonationalist Arrangements* is closely linked with the media logics and discursive functions of the first pattern, since this pattern also benefits from the production of controversy and distraction and the simplification and affective appeal that gender topics evoke. Moreover, as the openly sexist arguments of both Bolsonaro and Trump (and their endorsement on the part of their supporters), together with their rigid anti-immigration and pro militarization politics have shown, such masculinist practices serve the affective appeal of a strong and charismatic (and "classically/naturally" male) leader so central to populism. Gender topics enable these leaders to present themselves as part of the "normal" people as opposed to a "political correct gender police" that is threatening the lives and values of the "silent majority". Both presidents have, at least in part, continuously disavowed or withdrawn from the image of being sexist or homophobe. Both also rely on women like Trump's "liberal feminist" daughter Ivanka or Bolsonaro's family minister Alves, who represent ambiguous gender politics in order to distract attention from this dimension and keep those shocked by their masculinism "on board". This demonstrates how straightforward misogyny and racism cost votes in increasingly diverse societies. Thus, there is a need to temper, or at least blur, the sexist or homophobic accusations. On the other hand, this pattern shows that gender and sexual politics are effective tools for the mobilization of affects and for the re-ordering of social hierarchies through the re-naturalization of the binary, heteronormative order.

In order for this re-masculinization and re-establishment/maintenance and performed modernization of traditional gender hierarchies and sexual regimes to function, the logic of "femonationalist alliances" plays a crucial role. Femonationalist alliances describe the way women support right-wing populist politics and arguments, elaborating on the advantages such seemingly contradictory alliances bring the women. The examples of groups and individuals supportive of Trump and Bolsonaro have shown that one of their benefits is their recognition by right-wing populist males – these women are often rewarded with certain positions of power (usually not the highest ones). On the other hand, through the union with White supremacist males for the sake of the nation and the nuclear heteronormative family, these women can imagine themselves as "racially/ culturally" superior and already emancipated, as the above-mentioned commentaries on feminism as "sexist" or "anti-male" indicate. For that purpose, the construction of a common enemy such as "genderism"/ "gender ideology" and affirmative action as a challenge to the established order, the defense of a particular lifestyle and values as the norm, and as a form of privileging the wrong groups, fulfills a crucial function.

Hence, the third pattern *(White) Re-Masculinization: "Genderism" as Existential Threat* addresses the crucial role of the opposition to gender studies, gender approaches and LGBTQI activism for the right-wing populist nationalist and (often) nativist self-image. Again, gender provides an arena for the construction of a common enemy as an existential threat to the way of living and loving perceived as "normal" and to the "nation" or "people" as a whole. Instead of addressing the economic order as a source of inequality, the attack of the so-called "gender ideology" functions as a buffer for the perceived threats. The naturalization of the traditional binary and heteronormative gender regime thus discursively turns into a matter of "survival" for the nation.

Perceived as part of a "left" "liberal" discourse resulting from the social movements of the 1960s and 1970s and the related "sexual revolution", the so-called "gender ideology" and affirmative action are demonized as privileging undeserving minorities, and thus severely limiting the social mobility and access to success for the "native" majority that, in this mindset, rightfully, and naturally "deserves" them. More recently, this paradigm is also projected onto the global scale in the form of the reverse anti-colonial notion of "gender ideology as ideological colonization" introduced by the Vatican, uniting numerous conservative, right-wing populist and extremist forces in the struggle against this supposedly all-encompassing global threat.

Accordingly, with pattern four, *Reverse Anti-Colonialism: "Gender Ideology" as "Ideological Colonization"* we see the "natural" gender and social order threatened on a global scale by the "chaotic" and harmful "ideology" represented by gender. As the example of the fight against diversity in school education demonstrates, "normal" people become the victims of an imagined worldwide network of "gender ideologists" who seek to destroy the "natural" binary and heteronormative order and hence also the survival of the nuclear family and the nation. Pursuing a sort of *Reverse Anti-Colonialism*, radical conservative and right-wing actors position themselves as the victims of the "ideological" menace of gender. The construction of a global and all-encompassing threat enables a number of alliances between different radical conservative, right-wing populist and extremist groups and their female supporters, which is why I have termed this phenomenon of joined forces "femoglobal" alliances. The reverse anti-colonial struggle against "gender ideology" and the related femoglobal alliances are somewhat contradictory to the following pattern on *"Gender and/as 'Sexual Exceptionalism' and 'Intersectionality from Above'"*, since "sexual exceptionalism" is based on the self-narration as emancipated and being in possession of the more progressive gender and sexual regime. For some women, this narrative provides a way out of their "emancipation fatigue" that they have experienced as stressful and frustrating, while they gain from alliances with men on the basis on nationalism or nativism. However, as we have seen in various of the preceding examples – such as Trump's "I'm not a feminist, I'm for everyone" and his simultaneous sexist remarks and celebrations of "traditional" marriage – show that rightwing populism easily unites such contradictions and works via oscillating between a politics of "either/or" and "both … and". The above-mentioned phenomena, such as femonationalist (and other seemingly absurd) alliances, demonstrate that gendered right-wing populist discourse relies on and functions through these contradictions and paradoxes.

Pattern five *"Ethno-sexism" and "Exclusive Intersectionality" (Gendering of Social Inequalities and Gendering of Fear)* focuses on the "ethno-sexist" projection of sexism and "backward sexual" and gender regimes onto Muslim or immigrant Others (Trump's "Mexican rapists") and the related gain for right-wing populists and their femonationalist (and homonationalist) supporters alike. Thereby, the actual re-traditionalization of gender hierarchies can be combined with the narrative of modernization. This pattern simultaneously justifies the rejection of feminism and "genderism", since the populists position their own, national, group as being in possession of the superior sexual regime and thus already emancipated. It also makes plausible the anti-immigrant and anti-Muslim racisms which envision the "emancipatory backwardness" of these Others as a threat of the sexual freedom of the "autochthonous" women (and, sometimes, gays) and exclusionary practices of "exclusive intersectionality" in the form of rigid immigration politics and border regimes, in the name of women's (and gay) rights.

Gender serves a twofold function in right-wing populist discourse: on the one hand, following Sauer, gender is particularly useful for mobilizing a new common sense and a "new hegemonic compromise". The reference to gender allows populists to relate the long-standing sexual binary that still marks peoples' habits despite being "shattered" to equality politics: "The right-wing populist mobilization of gender thus points to the deeply en-gendered structuring of western societies which can easily be updated." (Sauer 2017, 14, translation JR) On the other hand, problematizing the gender orders of outsiders, which is also a populist construction of enemies, on the one hand serves to prove the "proper", Occidental superiority and "sexual exceptionalism" (Dietze 2016b). This order is opposed to the imagined "natural" or "cultural" sexism of the misogyny and homophobia of immigrants. Imaginations of the "untamed masculinity" of "other" men are part and parcel of this imaginary. They are instrumentalized for the outsourcing of emancipatory issues within the nation's own borders and simultaneously create a threat that justifies the exclusion of the thus perceived aggressor. Through this division, the borders and/or limits of citizenship and belonging are also negotiated. The related "simulated progressiveness" (Dietze 2017) serves simultaneously to play down the group's own emancipation deficits and maintain the traditional binary and heterosexual/-normative gender order and to co-opt women and gays for anti-immigration propaganda. Furthermore, those who have been fighting for and insisting on these rights, such as feminists and LGBTQI activists, are demonized as representing a threat to (heteronormative) families and the sexual binary, as well as to the (reproduction of the) nation. On the other hand, through the sense of community and superiority and the outsourcing of the threat to both "gender ideology" and "external rapists", attention is being distracted from the effects of globalization and social inequalities.

As the reading of the exemplary cases of Jair Bolsonaro and Donald Trump right-wing populist "communicative patterns" indicates, a gender perspective – or a focus on the workings of gender – serves to make the anti-pluralistic and anti-liberal project of right-wing populism visible. Thereby, it becomes workable, since a gender perspective reveals the tensions and contradictions in the right-wing populist discourse, such as those between class, nationality, and gender, which can then be critically examined. The entanglements of racism, ethnosexism (ethicizing sexism as a Muslim/immigrant mode) and sexism indicate that feminist, queer, anti-racist and intersectional scholarship is urgently required in the field of right-wing populism research. In light of such contradictions, Dietze (2015) rightfully stipulates that we must "read anti-genderism intersectionally" in order to grasp the different dimensions – of various and simultaneous axes of stratification and privilege that are usually constitutive – of the workings of gender for right-wing populist discourse in their complexity.

4.1. Table 1: Right-Wing Populist Patterns of En-Gendering

The following table aims to depict the ways in which gender aspects function within populist logics in order to propel certain right-wing populist discourses into broader public arenas:

Communicative Pattern	**Patterns of (En-)Gendering**	**Antagonistic Populist Logic**
Gendering of Scandals + ("ethnic") Others	**Gender as "Affective Bridge" in (Mass) Media**	**Emotional Appeal** **Simplicity of Argument** Facts vs. (Gender) Ideology
"Normal" people vs. politically correct gender police	**Appropriating Women's Politics for Femonationalist Arrangements**	(Re-)naturalization of binary roles, heteronormative order
(White) Re-Masculinization: Against "Gender Ideology" + Affirmative Action	"Genderism" as existential threat	"Genderism" + immigrants as scapegoats for inequalities + fears

Radical Religious and Femoglobal Alliances	Gender as "Ideological Colonization"	**Reverse Anti-Colonialism (Self-Victimization)** "Natural" order vs. "chaotic", menacing gender diversity
Gendering of Social Inequalities **Gendering of Fear**	"Ethno-Sexism" + "Exclusive Intersectionality"	**Sexual Exceptionalism** Superior vs. inferior sexual regimes Modernization + Retraditionalization

Source: (Roth 2019, cf. Ajanovic, Mayer and Sauer 2017, Diehl 2017, Dietze 2015, Mudde and Kaltwasser 2017, Sauer 2017)

While right-wing populists stand for the exclusive pattern of "intersectionality from above", feminist movements throughout the Americas, emerging simultaneously with the right-wing trend, confront this conservative backlash through manifold practices that might be called "intersectionality from below". These movements build on a long trajectory of female as well as feminist resistance, "intersectional" activist practices and theorizing and will be the focus of the second part of this study as contestations to the right-wing populist contestations.

Part II

5. Can Intersectional Feminism Trump Populism?

I am not free while any woman is a prisoner, even when her shackles are very different from my own.

—Final public words of Marielle Franco at Casa das Pretas, March 14, 2018

(T)he future of our earth may depend upon the ability of all women to identify and develop new definitions of power and new patterns of relating across differences.

—Audre Lorde from *Age, Race, Class, and Sex*

The first speaker at the Women's March in Washington D.C. in January 2017 paralleling Donald Trump's inauguration as president was the Latina actress with the paradigmatic name America Ferrera. Ferrera opened her powerful speech with a reference to her own experience as a female immigrant: "As a woman and as a proud first-generation American born to Honduran immigrants, it's been a heartbreaking time to be both a woman and an immigrant in this country. Our dignity, our character, our rights have all been under attack." – Ferrera did not limit her talk to her own personal experience, but rather took it as a point of departure to claim the rights of all marginalized and oppressed groups, ranging from Muslims, to LGBTI persons to African Americans, and immigrants – expressed also in her use of the "we". Positioning herself as speaking for and with all these minorities, Ferrera denied the new president the authority to represent and define "America":

> We are gathered here and across the country and around the world today to say, Mr. Trump, we refuse. We reject the demonization of our Muslim brothers and sisters. We condemn the systemic murder and incarceration of our black brothers and sisters. We will not ask our LGBT families to go backwards. We will not go from being a nation of immigrants to a nation of ignorance. We won't build walls and we won't see the worst in each other. (Ferrera 2017)

Ferrera's intervention paradigmatically emphasizes solidarity and coalition building across differences in order to critique and oppose nationalist and populist ideology and hegemony and to claim a coalition to confront multiple axes of oppression. Her strategically essentialist mobilization of the category "women" functions as a tool of politization for defending a pluralistic understanding of the imagined community "America".

*

Significantly, also many banners at the marches made reference to the necessity of "intersectionality" – a term formerly predominantly used in academic feminist contexts – e.g. in slogans such as "Feminism without Intersectionality isn't Feminism", or "If your Feminism isn't Intersectional who is it even for?", which reminded of Audre Lorde's famous phrase that "There is no such thing as a single-issue struggle, because we do not live single-issue lives" or Angela Davis' "I can't Imagine a Feminism that isn't Anti-Racist." Some older protesters were holding a sign saying, "I can't believe I'm still protesting this same shit!" on a T-Shirt worn by Women's March organizer Tamara Lee during the 2016 march, we could even read Sojourner Truth's famous phrase "Ain't I a Woman?" – which the formerly enslaved African American and women's rights activist had expressed during her legendary intervention at the Women's Conference in Akron, Ohio, in 1951 (see photographs in WMO 2018, 94).

New feminist movements had already before the Women's Marches been formed first in Argentina and then in Mexico against femicide, the structural violence and killing of women. The movement became nationally recognized with the use of the hashtag *#NiUnaMenos* on social media, title under which massive demonstrations were held on June 3, 2015, in Buenos Aires to protest the murder of 14-year-old Chiara Paez, found buried underneath her boyfriend's house a few weeks pregnant. The protests congregated around 200,000 people in Buenos Aires and extended to Uruguay and Chile. One year later, on June 3, 2016 the multitudinous demonstration took place once again throughout Argentina under the new slogan *#VivasNosQueremos* (#WeWantUsAlive), and the march was also replicated in Montevideo, Uruguay, Chile, and Peru. October 19, 2016 saw the *#NiUnaMenos* mass strike against femicide in Argentina, a large-scale response to the murder of 16-year-old Lucía Pérez, who was drugged and violated for being young and a woman. On posters carried at the marches one could read *Todas somos Lucía Pérez* (We Are All Lucía Pérez).

The protest intensified a year later, after Santiago Maldonado, a young activist for indigenous rights who took part in a road block in 2017, was missing after the Argentine police dispersed the demonstration. His body was later found drowned near a river, his disappearance had caused massive protests demanding the clarification of the circumstances of his disappearance and death. The case was examined as a possible "forced disappearance", which could not be proved. Similar demonstrations took place in other South American countries including Mexico, El Salvador, and Chile. A week later, on October 25, 2017, Brazil held its own *#NiUnaMenos* strike (Draper 2018, Lorey 2019). Under the motto *Ni Una Menos/Ni Una Más* (Not One Less/Not One More), the protesters denounce above all the structural violence against women and gender non conform people who are frequent victims of femicides and transvesticides and have since at least the mass protests for the right to abortion of 2018 gained greater visibility and influence (see Varias autoras 2017). In Brazil the protests following the murder of afro-descendant openly lesbian politician Marielle Franco under the banner *Marielle presente!* intensified after Bolsonaro's election and were accompanied by the *EleNão* and *Mulheres Contra Bolsonaro* campaigns. In the Latin American contexts in particular, the protests and strikes are based on profound critique of capitalism and the related gendered modes of production and division of labor. The rhetoric and semiotics of the protests is based on solidarity and alliances with poor women, workers, indigenous and immigrant women.

The recently increasing number of feminist movements indicates that right-wing gender politics also has opened up a renewed arena for resistance and counter-movements. The *Ni Una Menos* and *Ni Una Más* movements in Argentina and Mexico and many other parts of Latin America, the Women's March on Washington paralleling Donald Trump's presidential inauguration or most recently the protest by feminists in Brazil against the murder of Marielle Franco and the candidacy of Jair Bolsonaro were manifestations of broad coalitions of protest to the white supremacist, sexist and homophobic backlashes we currently observe in many places. Also, in Germany, the marches by AfD women led to broad strategic alliances. In Washington and Berlin and many other places, the protests were expressions of a heretofore unforeseen decidedly "intersectional" notion of feminism. Also, in the arts, we currently observe a number of initiatives and expressions of resistance and mobilizations. Since the International Women's Strike on March 8, 2017, 2018 and 2019, these movements show an even stronger emphasis of the entanglement of gender violence and inequalities with economic power structures and the systemic character of such violence and oppression.

Feminist movements are in full swing in many places and struggle for new spaces in order to make their claims publicly heard. The hashtag #MeToo – which the protesters at these strikes turned into a collective "#WeToo" – documents the global system of sexualized violence against women in all its articulations, which the activists of the *Ni Una Menos* movement all over Latin America also contest vehemently. However, in contrast to online feminist practices – which have undoubtedly become crucial spaces for feminist organizing for all mentioned groups (and more) – the current protests are marked by the fact that they are uniting actual bodies in the streets. While numerous radical right-wing actors have also begun to publicly express their positions in many places and spaces, the feminist movements resist and contest the right-wing turn and the related exclusive power structures that made it possible. The numerous clear and strong reference to their predecessors in the mentioned examples of women's and feminist interventions show that the fight against multiple and interrelated scales or levels of oppression is not new, but dates back to a long tradition of feminist activist intervention. (For instance, Brah and Phoenix (2004), Hearn (2011), Zapata Galindo (2011), Viveros Vigoya (2013), and Brah (2013) remind us that black feminists and anti-slavery movements already by the 18th and 19th centuries and "probably before then" claimed the recognition of their racist discrimination (Hearn 2011, 90).)

Against this background, this second part of the study asks "what feminism can do" with regard to counter-strategies to right-wing populism, closed borders, and racism, and for alternative visions of the social. It asks what these movements' politics, strategies and visions are, and how they position themselves in relation to prior movements and their feminist and anti-racist predecessors. This part of the study is also interested in examining the role of bringing bodies together on the streets to form an oppositional collective "we".

As will be argued in what follows, the new feminist movements on the one hand represent one of the most powerful and visible forces of opposition to the worldwide radical right-wing trend. On the other hand, the activists are responsive to their feminist activist "ancestors" throughout the hemisphere, to whom many of the slogans and politics refer. Thereby, the current movements seemingly re-connect the concept of intersectionality to its radical and activist roots and transform it into concrete political practices. In order to pay credit to the long tradition of intersectional and transnational feminist politics of connectedness, the following section will give a short overview of exemplary relational forms of resistances, alliances and movements by women and feminists. The study will then elaborate on the current expression and future outlooks of intersectional feminist practices as a contestation and a counterbalance to right-wing populist politics, focusing on exemplary publications, media coverage, talks, interviews, and personal conversations.

5.1. Resisting Colonial Entanglements and En-Genderings in Early Feminisms

The Americas have a "shared, but divided" history (Randeria 2006 [1999]) that is marked by coloniality, decolonization, migration, diaspora experiences and plurality and diversity. Against this backdrop, the societies of the Americas can resort to a long experience of dealing with differences and inequalities, but also with resistance against exploitation, oppression, enslavement and imperialism. Inter-American processes of exchange have been structurally marked by an "intersectional" – ethnicized, racialized, en-gendered, colonial – dimension. The Americas also share a long history of struggles over who belongs to and represents "America" – be it the US or other nation states throughout the region – and who is entitled to have full citizenship rights and access to freedom, human rights, resources, participation and social mobility. Numerous examples of resistance by indigenous inhabitants, enslaved laborers and women demonstrate that struggles have always implied a certain "intersectional" dimension due to the deeply racialized and (en)gendered structure of the hierarchies and inequalities implemented with colonialism. And women of marginalized groups were often at the forefront. As Verene Shepherd (2008) illustrates, enslaved women in the Caribbean had been opposing their dehumanization, exploitation and enslavement from the outset. In various ways in form of practices ranging from restraining their daughters from missionary schools, and continuing to confront violent and sexploitative masters, to maroonage (*cimarronaje* in Spanish), participation in abolitionist groups and protest songs, they resisted the system all the way from the slave ports of the African West Coast throughout the existence of the regime of slavery (137). All over the Americas – above all in the US, the Caribbean, Central America and Brazil – numerous enslaved women also escaped and lived in hiding or as cimarronas in maroon societies, while others practiced birth strikes (139). Abolition also had a deep inter-American dimension. Several feminist movements and practices emerged at the same time, while others pursued feminist aims long before the term or the movement existed.

Soon after the French Revolution (1789), the freedom fighters who built the first independent Latin American state in Saint-Domingue (today Haiti) pointed out the contradiction between ideas of human rights and freedom and the system of institutionalized enslavement. Around the same time, feminists like Olympe de Gouges (France 1791) and Mary Wollstonecraft (Great Britain 1792) highlighted the fact that the newly introduced "human rights" were limited to white male citizens. At the Women's Rights Convention in Akron, Ohio (USA 1851), Sojourner Truth in her speech *Ain't I a Woman?* questioned the universality of white bourgeois feminism by pointing out her experience as a black and formerly enslaved woman. In her statement at the Women's rights Convention in 1851, Sojourner Truth anticipated the problematic of differences between women, as well as the entanglement of class, racialization and gender – which also forms the basis on which intersectional practices and theorizing is built.

Despite the "shared" part of their history, that of social stratification, intersectional en-gendered and racialized processes of ordering and hierarchization have been articulated in locally very diverse forms in the Americas as part of the implementation of capitalist logics of production and the related unequal gendered and racialized division of labor. Under the rigid racist regime of plantation slavery, a structure of racist hierarchization dominated in the US that Vilna Bashi Treitler has termed "Ethnic Project" (Bashi Treitler 2013), and according to which Whites are always positioned at the top and Blacks at the bottom of the racial pyramid in the US. Since the 19th century the focus shifted towards the "racial quartet" (Dietze 2013), which was expanded to the gender dimension, and is marked by a strong competition between racial and gendered politics (White male – White female – Black male – Black female). "Other", e.g. indigenous or Latina positions simultaneously experienced a further marginalization. In large parts of Latin America, multi-level, ethnisized and racialized gender hierarchies emerged (e.g. between *criol-*

los, *mestizos*, *negros*, *indígenas*), on the top of which was always the (White) man of European origin (see Wade 2009). By now, the discourse has shifted more strongly towards "backwards" gender roles (of non-Europeans) which according to a colonial Eurocentric development narrative should optimize following the model of (North-West) Europe.

5.2. Trajectories: Shared Experiences, Feminist Networks and Alliances

Numerous feminist networks between Latin America, the Caribbean and the US were built, e.g., in the context of transnational, and imperial feminisms emerging between 1840-1880, and, later, in form of international feminist co-operations in the context of the International Conferences of American States 1880-1948. However, conventional narratives of the emergence of the feminist movements in the Americas focus on the US and the Seneca Falls meeting. Most works separate feminist politics from anti-racist or class struggles, and also different feminisms from one another, thus marginalizing the connected histories and genealogies and the simultaneous articulation of diverse feminist politics in the Americas.

The experience of being refused the participation in the World Anti-Slavery Convention in London in 1840 fueled the conviction of White US feminists Elizabeth Cady Stanton and Lucretia Mott to found the Women's Movement at the Seneca Falls Convention in 1848 which was marked by transnational events such as the simultaneous US-Mexican war (see Moynagh 2012, Stanley Holten 2010). According to Gabriele Dietze (2013), abolitionism forms the backdrop against which feminism unfolded in the US, and feminism actually emerged from abolitionism (45).

Women abolitionists fought the slave trade and plantation slavery also in the West Indies and Latin America. Feminists from South and North America intervening in the International Conferences of American States in the late 19th and early 20th centuries (1880-1948) provide an insightful example of transnational feminist practices and politics. Already before official international feminist meetings were held and feminists started intervening in international conferences, women resisted their oppression and exploitation and exchanged ideas and strategies across and beyond national borders in the Americas (see Moynagh 2012, Roth 2018 and 2019).

Despite numerous tensions, inequalities, and conflicts within and between the different groups, the majority of the so-called first wave of feminisms in the Americas of the 19th century was generally dedicated to a strategy and politics of "global sisterhood" in order to claim basic human and civil rights such as suffrage and participation in international institutions (see Roth 2019). However, from the outset numerous feminists of color such as Sojourner Truth had addressed the missing racial and class solidarity. Feminist claims and positions diversified gradually in the course of the so-called second wave during the following decades, which, once basic rights like suffrage were achieved, were marked by the diversification of claims and positions. The feminist movements of the Civil Rights Era in the US fought one of the strictest and most openly segregated racial regimes based on blatant racial inequalities, whereas many Latin American countries faced dictatorships and civil wars during this period. By pointing at the "whitewashing" of the so-called second wave feminism, Benita Roth claims that the Chicana/Latina and Black Feminist movements in the USA have not formed as a reaction to white feminists' ignorance and racism (see Roth 2004). Rather, different feminisms emerged around the same time in dialogue with and as a reaction to but also part of leftist male movements and feminist movements. Distinct feminist groups have formed simultaneously along the lines of singular-gender oppression versus multiple oppressions and mutually influenced each other. Facing such interlocking systems of oppression, transnational inter-American exchange continued in the Americas.

5.3. From the Civil Rights Movement to the Women's March on Washington

More than a century after Sojourner Truth gave her famous speech, the *Manifesto das Mulheres Negras* (1975) in Brazil and the Combahee River Collective Statement (1979) in the USA, provided decisive interventions into dominant feminist representations, pointing to the entangled and interdependent character of different forms of oppression. Angela Davis (1981) referred to the interrelated hierarchies of women, race, and class in a book with the same name. Chicana feminists like Gloria Anzaldúa and Cherrie Moraga coined the concept of the "Borderland" as a concrete physical space (the US-Mexican border), but also to define a "Chicana identity" based on being located between various cultures. It is intended to represent ambiguous spaces and identities beyond established binary categories and signifies a new form of creating and understanding knowledge. In a similar way, Caribbean feminist artists and thinkers have stressed the close entanglement between racialized, gendered and classed hierarchies on account of the global inequalities produced by colonial hierarchies, the legacies of enslavement and the persistent "North-South" exploitation. Non-hegemonic feminists like Patricia Hill Collins, bell hooks, Audre Lorde, June Jordan, Norma Alarcón, Chela Sandoval, Chandra Talpade Mohanty, Sylvia Wynter, María Lugones, and many more have followed a similar agenda, and early on insisted and elaborated on entangled dimensions of oppression and inequality (Roth 2004).

In 1981, non-state/"extra-official" gatherings such as those known as Latin American and Caribbean Feminist *Encuentros*, began to be held, the first decade of which was marked by the negotiation of politics and the production of feminist identities. Largely, the participants of the *Encuentros* put emphasis on the prospects for forging alliances across regional feminist movements based on minimum common values and goals. Interventions and theorizing by African-American, Chicana, working-class, Communist, and lesbian and queer feminists – such as the Combahee River Collective, Angela Davis, Toni Morrison, Kimberlé Crenshaw, bell hooks, Patricia Hill Collins in the US, and the *Mulheres Negras Brasileiras*, the Zapatista Women of Chiapas or the collective Afrocubanas in Latin America and the Caribbean, to name but a few – contributed enormously to an interlocking understanding of different inequalities and the simultaneity (rather than the consecutive formation) of different strands of feminist practices and politics.

Recently, Latin American feminist groups like the collective *Mujeres Creando* in Bolivia provide another example of alliances of solidarity between differently positioned women from urban lesbians to rural poor and indigenous women. Moreover, the diverse feminisms that have marked the Americas make a claim for creating solidarity. They further demand the inclusion of cultural practices and artefacts as sites of politics and of knowledge production and circulation in order to represent and reach a wider spectrum of contexts and experiences and confronting multiple intersecting forms of exclusion and oppression. As we have seen, the current feminist movements can rely on a long trajectory of feminist resistance to the shared experiences of oppression, exclusion and violence.

6. Recent Revivals of Intersectional Practices in New Feminist Movements

6.1. The Women's Marches

Initially starting as an online forum, the Women's March was from the outset aimed at uniting resistant bodies together in the streets. The idea for a women's march on Washington was born in viral Facebook posts put up after the 2016 election independently by Bob Bland, one of the current co-chairwomen, and Teresa Shook, a retired lawyer in Hawaii, who soon joined forces. Before any logistical arrangements had been made, tens of thousands of women committed to travel to Washington on social media. Some of the women making initial preparations realized it would be a disaster if the march seemed to be entirely by and for White women. They thus brought African American Tamika Mallory and Chicana Latina Carmen Pérez, both affiliated with the NGO Gathering for Justice, on board, who, in turn, brought in Palestinian American Linda Sarsour. The original idea to name the demonstration "Million Women's March" was abandoned after harsh critique, since it copied the title of the "Million Women's March" of 1997 in Philadelphia which had focused on bringing together Women of Color. As director of operations and national organizer Vanessa Wruble recounts (WMO 2018, 37), the team decided to call the protest the "Women's March on Washington" instead, as an homage to the 1963 march for the civil and freedom rights of African Americans which united civil rights, labor and religious organizations and where Martin Luther King held his famous *I had a Dream* speech to end racism. The organizing team put the first Women's March together in just 10 weeks with the aim of mobilizing as many people as possible in opposition to the politics represented by Donald Trump under a common banner. Like most social movements, the March did not start from a concrete political program.

Singer Alicia Keys opened her "warm-up" speech at the march quoting the famous poem *And Still I Rise* (1978) by African America poet Maya Angelou. In her contribution to the book *Together We Rise* by the Woman's March organizers (and Condé Nast) (WMO 2018), Keys expresses the refusal of state bio politics over female, Black and other precarious bodies: "We will not allow our bodies to be owned and controlled by men in government or men anywhere" (Alicia Keys, cf. in WMO 2018, 211). The book's title also references the famous Angelou, and the preface also gives credit to the powerful legacy of women of color:

> We also want to shine a light on the women-of-color-led resistance work that continues to be done across the country and that is so critical to our democracy and our humanity. When women lead, a different narrative emerges, one of collaboration – in which rather than being divided by race, sexual orientations ability, or other factors, we are united, bringing all our identities to bear in favor of fundamental human equality. (WMO 2018, 12)

Maya Angelou's poem is also prominently quoted in the first lines of the introduction to the volume by writer and activist Jamia Wilson, who celebrates the achievements of Black feminism and supports the Women's March's dedication to these predecessors. Wilson also emphasizes the power of art and poetry as part of what she defines as "the resistance":

> 'You may shoot me with your words, you may cut me with your eyes, you may kill me with your hatefulness. But still, like air, I rise.'
>
> Poet, feminist and racial justice advocate Maya Angelou wrote these words 40 years ago, long before a group of visionary women (many of whom had not yet been born) ignited the movement we now know as the resistance. The passion and determination of this small group brought Angelou's proclamation to life. Rise we did. (Wilson 2018, 13)

The title of the book – *Together We Rise* – already creates a strategic discursive "we" that includes many voices and bodies. In unity, *together*, all these bodies "rise" and thus resist, contest, become visible. The dedication to the book also emphasizes the unifying character of the march and the movement and represents a claim for solidarity and its intersectional scale – unlike right-wing populist rhetoric that includes only "polite" or only certain women: "Dedicated to women, documented and undocumented: The daughters, the caregivers, the workers, the trans warriors, the witches, the artists, the refugees, the leaders. You are our light in the dark." (7) The long legacy/trajectory of feminist foremothers and role models is also evoked by the names of the women listed in Ai-Jen Poo's contribution, which includes "Sojourner Truth, Susan B. Anthony, Ella Baker, Sylvia Rivera, Audre Lorde, Wilma Mankiller, and Dorothy Bowen" (Poo 2018, 69). And so does the photo showing four protestors holding posters with the portraits of famous women's rights activists from different times, in the front of which a little Black girl holds a poster saying, "My Future Matters" (WMO 2018, 207). The view that the present must be aware of the past in order to re-invent the future is also expressed in sister Aisha Al-Asawiya's essay *Sankofa: Look Back to Move Forward* (WMO 2018, 73) in which she states that "[i]n order to know where you are going, you have to know where you are coming from" (74), while feminist activist and Black Power icon Angela Davis expressed it in more Marxist terms: "We are collective agents of history" (Davis 2017). Davis closed her speech at the march with a call to struggle, claiming that "[t]he next 1,459 days of the Trump administration will be 1,459 days of resistance" (ibid.). In numerous of the contributions (to the book and the march), the power of collective action is further emphasized. Cecile Richards, president of the Planned Parenthood Federation of America, for instance, claimed that: "one of us can be dismissed. Two of us can be ignored. But together we are a movement and we are unstoppable" (Richards, cf. in WMO 2018, 65). And Jenny Munro, a Wirad Juri elder and human rights campaigner, underlines the mutual interconnectedness of all women and community members, which goes against the grain of rapid individualism and isolated "single issue" identity politics: "if a woman suffers, we all suffer. And believe you me, my people and my women have suffered." (Munro, cf. in WMO 2018, 37). The list of (official/institutional) participant organizations of the March demonstrates the manifold fields from which the protesters come, ranging from environmental justice activism to LGBTQI and immigrant rights (WMO 2018, 297-306). Based on this broad, and intersectional character, these new movements seemingly represent a new dimension of resistance to the current right-wing trends. Going back to a long legacy of intersectional resistance, this part of the study is interested in discussing the function of these new decidedly intersectional coalitions as an avant-garde for imagining new forms of the social.

Women's March Strategic Adviser and National Organizer Sarah Sophie Flicker points out that the Black Lives Matter movement, which had already been actively protesting for some time, is a crucial predecessor: "The Women's March wouldn't have happened without all the amazing organizing of Black Lives Matter, BLM was training American people to get out on the streets and stay out on the streets for years before the Women's March came out" (Flicker, WMO 2018, 236). Cassady Fendlay (Fendlay 2019) further names the Spanish movement Podemos as one of the major sources of inspiration for the Women's March, as well as the Occupy movement, in which many of the later Women's March organizers had been involved.

Throughout the book *Together We Rise*, the authors also emphasize the importance of physically protesting in the streets and building a collective body – unlike in social media campaigns where you just push a button, "like", or sign a petition.

The diversity – or multitude – of participating actors also points to the fact that the movement is contesting more than the current presidents and their governments, addressing the very structures that are founded on the constitutive exclusion or constitutive unevenness that Laclau (2005, 118) considers foundational for populism in certain demographics, of certain precarious bodies. This position is also expressed in phrases like the one by feminist author, academic and journalist Roxane Gay, who asks "How do we fight for ourselves while also fighting for the greater good? How do we hold ourselves accountable?" (Gay 2018, 288).

The "Unity Principles" that can be found both in the book (107) and on the Women's March website (under the title Global Unity Principles) – encompassing environmental justice, immigrant rights, disability rights, civil rights, workers' rights, LGBTQI rights, reproductive rights, and ending violence – are meant to frame a broad multitude of positions.

6.1.1. Orchestrating Bodies and Struggles: "Pussy Hats"

Photo no. 5: Amandalynn Jones. A woman cheers during the Madison WI rally for the Women's March on January 21, 2017. Wikimedia Commons.

Visually, this inclusivity or politics of "unity in diversity" was also expressed by the pink "pussy hats" many protesters wore to oppose Trump's sexist comments. In her contribution to *Together We Rise*, Krista Suh, inventor of the hats, asks "How could I predict how many hats there would be?" (2018, 257) when she knitted the first model that would be copied thousands and thousands of times. Suh emphasizes the unifying character of the emblematic accessory: "The pussy hat has gotten criticism, but that's fine with me. It represents something greater than a pink hat. The pussy hat shows you're not alone" (ibid.). The pussy hat is obviously an ironic citation of

Donald Trump's misogynist phrase from the Hollywood Tapes, in which he claimed that as a powerful man he is entitled to "grab" women "by the pussy". By performing as the "pussies" – and thus re-appropriating this position – and claiming public space, the protesters contest and reject the violent heteronomy over women's bodies. A similar reversal could also be seen in posters reading "Grab them by the patriarchy" distributed by the Democrats Abroad at the 2017 March in Berlin and elsewhere.

Knitting instructions for the pussy hats were soon widely circulated, and thus their production was turned into a communal and pop-cultural feminist practice. The hats can also be purchased on the internet from the trademark "Pussyhat Project" under the header "Design Intervention for Social Change", whose mission is "advancing women's rights and human rights through the arts, education and respectful dialogue." The "Pussyhat Project™ Global Outreach" statement from February 18, 2017 lists the creation of a "concrete, accessible, thoughtful way for those who cannot attend activism events in person to be heard and represented", "developing meaningful, respectful connections among people who care about women's rights", and "creating a framework for community and personal agency from the local to the national level" (see Pussyhat Project 2017). Under the pink headgear, the march thus brought together people and groups opposing manifold forms of exclusion and oppression, among them LGBTQI activists, Muslim feminists, representatives of the Jewish community and, particularly, of the Black Lives Matter movement. These included Sybrina Fulton, the mother of Trayvon Martin, who had become a victim of police racism, who also called for collective and concerted action: "All our sons are in heaven and we continue to fight for our children (...) We are going to continue to fight. We've come too far now to turn back" (Fulton, cf. in WMO 2018, 281).

Alyssa Klein sees one of the achievements of the Women's March movement in its politicization of notions of intersectionality in order to unite struggles and create solidarity for audiences traditionally not involved in theoretical academic debates:

> Where Women's March plays a role in the bigger picture is to take concepts in activism and organizing and to make them as accessible as possible to the entire country. What we wanted to do was making intersectionality understandable for everyone and take this scholarly concept and make it part of everything that all of us do, not just as part of the population – at least everyone who believes in fighting for the greater good. That was something we started before the march and we've continued to do since. (Klein, cf. in WMO 2018, 274)

For a moment, the Women's march protesters brought the politics of intersectionality back onto the streets and to its activist roots, effecting a long-overdue transference from the academic ivory towers back to political practice. Intersectionality theoretician Kimberlé Crenshaw describes seeing all the different issues united under the Women's March banner and represented in the Pussy Hats as "the embodiment of the intersectional sensibilities that a lot of us have been working on for a very long time" (Crenshaw, cf. in Hess 2017). Bob Bland, the Women's March co-chairwoman, admits that she didn't know the concept when the organizing started, but now she deploys it often to emphasize the growing diversity of the March. It is in this way that the concept became a useful tool for the march on Washington, which set about the task of uniting feminism's mainstream, popular arm and its dissenting factions in only two months (Hess 2017).

The fact that the pink pussy hat made it to the February 2017 cover of the prestigious weekly Time magazine demonstrates the headgear's emblematic character and symbolism as well as the growing visibility and public impact of the movement and its claims. Given the initially spontaneous character of the march and the diversity of positions participating in it, the question soon arose of how sustainable the movement could be. As Hess affirms, the 2017 Women's March was one of the largest mass demonstrations in American history, uniting a broad range of groups that were all alarmed by Trump's election under one roof. For Crenshaw, the "million-dollar question" hence was whether these feminisms could survive under the anti-Trump umbrella (Crenshaw, cf. in Hess 2017).

6.1.2. From March to Movement

The potential to turn into a broader movement became obvious nine days after the first 2017 March, when masses of protesters gathered at airports to protest after Trump had implemented the "Muslim ban" for seven countries, six of them Muslim-majority. Some of the organizers consider the airport protest as a decisive step towards something more than a one-time event march. "The airport protest was the first victory of the resistance", commented Director of Social Media Strategy and National Organizer of the Women's March Alyssa Klein. "The Women's March was important as a symbol of resistance, but it wasn't a win in the sense of changing policy. The airport protest made a tangible impact." (Klein, cf. in WMO 2018, 236) Similar actions took place against Trump's attacks on affordable health care, against the illegalization of the Dreamers when Trump threatened to scrap the DACA program (Deferred Action for Childhood Arrivals), and against the National Rifle Association (NRA) (see Walters 2017). In February 2017 in a New York Times article titled *How a Fractious Women's Movement Came to Lead the Left* Amanda Hess emphasized the unifying character of the Women's March for the US American left, but also pointed to the momentous character of demonstrations that need to institutionalize in order to turn into more enduring movements. Former director of communications for the Women's March Cassady Fendlay emphasizes that the movement is more than the actual marches and online bubbles and is also "no anti-Trump movement" (Fendlay 2018). As the activities launched by Women's March organizers show, the movement soon became engaged in a variety of institution and policy building practices and also builds on prior movements.

As several contributions in the Women's March book *Together We Rise* indicate, the process and practice of "concerted action" is far from easy and requires the constant negotiation of conflicts. One of the obstacles and pitfalls the march organizers faced and still face is organizing in the times of social media, as the section titled *Spring 2017: Can Social Media Change the World?* discusses

(WMO 2018, 271). On the one hand, social media can help to organize many people in a short time span to gain great visibility. The contribution by Jamia Wilson ascribes the March's – at least momentary – "revolutionary" impact to social media when she observes that "on January 21, the revolution was televised, tweeted, and live-streamed, but flashed by in what felt like a second" (Wilson 2018, 16). Simultaneously, the Women's March – like other protests – is an indicator for and an expression of the need for other forms of organizing, as Women's March honorary co-chair and feminist legend Gloria Steinem pointed out: "Sometimes we must put our bodies where our beliefs are. Sometimes pressing send is not enough." (Steinem, cf. in WMO 2018, 97)

The protests also inspired the conservative and radical right side, however, as can be observed when accessing the comments on Fox News, in conservative blogs or pro-Trump Tweets, where the demonstrations are presented in form of an opposition narrative (Hess 2017). After the march, Fox News mocked clips of rally speeches, while Breitbart published photos with the headline "See what a massive, Hillary shaped bullet America just dodged?" (ibid.). The right-wing Media Research Center presented its collection of the most "vile and ridiculous signs", and Palestinian American Women's March organizer Linda Sarsour was besieged with anti-Muslim attacks on Twitter and Facebook. Meanwhile, the protestors of the "Pro-life" annual March for Life, who arrived at the Mall in Washington to demonstrate against abortion rights, were called "the real women's march" by *The Blaze*, indicating that the creation of two different realities and media perception bubbles are under way, as Seeßlen (2017) had described with regard to Trump supporters.

Hess (2017) was surprised that all the protesters gathered under the umbrella of a march for women, since only two months earlier, the left appeared fragmented and divided over the reasons for Hillary Clinton's electoral loss. Some said Clinton had ignored poor rural areas of the White working class or pushed other candidates out of the field, others made identity politics responsible for making White working-class voters feel excluded or blamed Whites for not mobilizing their relatives in the "heartland" (ibid.). Only when Hillary Clinton lost the election did popular feminism experience a crisis, as the voting results brought the fractures between different groups of women to the fore: 53 percent of White women voted for Trump, suggesting that many Americans were not opposed to misogyny. The result also pointed to the pitfalls of pure identity-politics-based notions of feminism, since, as Hess states, it "burst the bubble of cheery pop feminism, which had achieved its huge popularity at the expense of class consciousness and racial solidarity." (ibid.) While the left hence seemed severely divided in the fall of 2016, the Women's March came to provide a platform of unity, and, what is more, bring about a more "intersectional" conscience.

In 2019, two years after the first march, numerous voices, including New York Times columnist Michelle Goldberg (2019) drew the rather pessimistic – but perhaps untimely? – conclusion that the movement had failed. These voices accused the organizers of the March of having fallen short of building power once they were put at the top of a mass movement and of having alienated many supporters. "It's painful to see the Women's March fall apart now, but maybe it was always destined to be a moment instead of a movement." (ibid.) The 2019 Women's March was split over accusations of anti-Semitism, resulting in two distinct marches in New York City. Goldberg sees the splitting of the March following accusations of anti-Semitism against organizer Linda Sarsour and several others as the result of the uncoordinated organizing typical of social media, where content and political differences are often subsumed under simple slogans and based on protesting what one is "against", regardless of common ground with the other participants. "The Women's March ultimately faced a problem endemic to protest movements that organize spontaneously on the internet, going back to Occupy Wall Street." (ibid.) Goldberg argues that mass protest used to require deep, sustained organizing, with all the compromise and human connection that entailed, but has now been rendered obsolete through digital organizing. As a consequence, "people are often left trying to create a movement after a high-profile action, rather than before it, without clear common goals or leaders who have broadly accepted legitimacy." (ibid.)

6.1.3. Formulating Claims: The Women's Agenda 2019

Former director of communications for the Women's March Cassady Fendlay draws a more positive balance after the first two years of the movement and asserts: "If we are going to work together and keep on sharing strategies, we're going to work this out" (Fendlay 2018). Fendlay had before been a labor organizer and activist against police brutality, and joined the movement in 2017 for the March. From the start until 2018, Fendlay was director of communications for the Women's March, and she coordinated the process leading to the "Agenda" published in 2019.

Based on her experience as an organizer, Fendlay sees social media as a powerful tool for direct communication with an unprecedented outreach, but considers it "a terrible organizing tool" and confesses that she is "still a fan of one-to-one conversations" (ibid.). Nevertheless, when right-wing media takes things out of context (e.g. the vilification of Muslim women), social media can be a tool for creating a counter space and "[maybe] […] more social intelligence […] [for] changing the frame of critically evaluating information" (ibid.). She sees a danger in the right-wing opposition's strategy of demonizing and destroying all dissident voices, as could be seen in the case of the accusation of anti-Semitism against Women's March organizer Linda Sarsour: "now we've got all these wonderful people elected, but every time we present strong leaders, they will tear them down." (ibid.) The main motivation here is the "sense of emergency that gets created through the game of the White supremacist system and keeps us in crisis, in emergency" (ibid.). Despite these obstacles, she remains battle-ready. Fendlay reports that the Women's March in April 2019 relied on a decentralized network in 30 states across the US. "We began as a spontaneous protest, but quickly moved to put something together with intention" (ibid.). Fendlay was responsible for the organization of the

Agenda "process", in which ten issue areas were pulled out of the Unity Principles and ten committees built. The advisory council consisted of the original creators of the Unity Principles, interested in extending the vision of the "type of government we would like to have" (ibid.). The financing is still "very grassroots", the Agenda process, for example, counted on the support of NYU's Wagner students, since Fendlay was the only paid staff member, working an average of 80 hours a week. The plan was to look at the many intersections that should be achieved through the intentional table-building for each community (women of color, women with disabilities etc.). Each community chose two most urgent policies to be included in the Agenda.

On the Women's March website, the 2019 Women's Agenda is represented under the hashtag "#Womenswave" and the announcement "We're putting our collective influence to work in the halls of power" (Women's March 2019). The introduction claims that "Our intersectional feminist policy agenda is the first of its kind", and the introductory text underlines the necessity of sustainable social movements in times of political crisis like the present one and emphasize the need for social movements to confront the crisis:

> Historically, protest movements are difficult to sustain. (...) In this moment of U.S. history, one that will likely be written books about as among the darkest ones, we have lost the judicial and executive branches of government along with the Senate. Social movements are the only bulwark against the rising tide of authoritarianism, misogyny, white nationalism, racism, anti-Semitism, homophobia, transphobia, xenophobia, Islamophobia, ableism, classism, and ageism. (ibid.)

Referencing Kimberlé Crenshaw, who had introduced the concept of intersectionality to confront the juridical dilemma of intersecting axes of oppression such as racism and sexism, the Agenda lists its program as decidedly intersectional:

> Today, we advocate for an expansive understanding of intersectionality when we fight for social and policy change. This means,

> for instance, understanding that the problem of access to health care looks different for black women, trans women, disabled women and Indigenous women, and thus policies that address health care must take into account these different impacts and experiences. We believe the Women's Agenda is the first intersectional feminist policy platform. Women's March convened a group of 70 movement leaders to create this set of 24 essential federal policy priorities that form the foundation of the 2019 Women's March on Washington and will establish the priorities of our movement over the next two years. (ibid.)

The Women's March states as "Our Mission" – "to create a new future for this country, one where we are all free, equal, and safe." (Women's March 2019). The activities include a "Youth Empower" program with over 200 youth-led chapters nationwide, while a program on "Online Advocacy" claims that the Women's March Network is "an online advocacy program to fight the delegitimization of democracy online." (ibid.) The website further lists groups within the network that have formed over the past two years and were engaged consistently in opposing "the rising tide of state violence that threatens women across the country and the world", including the mobilization for the "A Day Without A Woman" strike in March 2017, a march to demand an end to gun violence, or the organization of the Women's Convention in Detroit in October 2017. In 2018, the network launched Power to the Polls, mobilized to demand an end to family separation of immigrants at the US-Mexican border, and organized a month of sustained actions as part of the campaign to #CancelKavanaugh, the candidate for Supreme Court Justice accused of sexually harassing several women. Following the website, the network maintained a consistent commitment to a phone program that focused on woman-to-woman voter contact in 2018 in order to motivate women to vote in the midterm elections and entertains the "Women's March Media Channel" in which they share the real-life stories of a diverse group of organizers and activists on the ground (ibid.). The Agenda demonstrates that numerous institution building, and consolidation practices are underway in the context of the Women's March organizers and activists, promising long-term activities.

6.1.4. International Networks and Broader Impact

Asked how the movements relate to the system and what role a critique of capitalism plays for them, Fendlay (2018) states that "we reject to be part of the system which is built on exclusionary principles. Our vision is transformative, a world that looks pretty different from our current world." And she continues, "we are certainly not pro the capitalist system as it stands, since the capitalist system is built on inequalities". However, she states that since "violence is happening today that we need to address while we work to change the system (…) we do have to do what we have to do today" (ibid.). One of the strategies she endorses is to try to get people into the Congress and to change the system, even though she is aware that "the two-party system is not good for what we want" (ibid.). In March 2018, there was already strong engagement in endorsing candidates for the 2018 midterm elections, including women of diverse backgrounds, who reflect progressive values. The Women's March organizers supported strong grassroots candidates in ten "battle states" in the form of face-to-face touring, trainings in voter registration and confronting oppressions. For Fendlay, it was hence particularly important to include the voices of the women most affected and traditionally secluded from feminist movements, such as indigenous women. She emphasizes that, since the midterm elections in 2018, for the first time in history two indigenous women are in Congress (ibid.). Fendlay admits that there has so far been no formal conversation with Latin American feminist movements, but that "we are in solidarity, fight for common goals" (Fendlay 2019). She sees the stronger emphasis on an anti-capitalist stance in the current Latin American movements as stemming from "a different language because of their unique social history." Fendlay emphasizes that the Women's March organizers try to be "intentionally anti-colonialist" and involve indigenous and Puerto Rican feminists (Puerto Rico is still a territory of the US).

Sophia Andary, Leader of Women's March San Francisco, when asked about their contact and dialogue with other women's rights organizations outside the USA, hesitates: "Hmm (…) I would say outside the USA not that much, only because with all honesty right now since Trump, since he took over, it has been non-stop work. It is really hard to focus on anything except local rights, national and local" (Andary 2018). Andary also underscores that intersectional feminism has to "look at the global status as well and has to actually truly care about what happens to a woman in the Middle East, or what happens to the women in Mexico or other parts of the country, and not just to women, what happens to people in struggle?" (ibid.). Andary considers the experience of participating in the Women's March as "a great way to empower women to step up, and it was also a great way to empower women that had never been involved to actually say 'I have a voice and I need to make sure my voice is heard'" (ibid.). However, she is also aware of the tensions and conflicts that have accompanied the movement from the outset, starting with the aforementioned circumstance that the movement was an initiative by White women who wanted to use a term taken from a historically African American protest, which set in motion the debate on the "urgency of intersectionality" (Crenshaw) (see Crenshaw's TED talk "The Urgency of Intersectionality" on the double invisibilization of the female African American victims).

Andary considers the Women's March movement a particularly suitable platform for "actual progression and intersectional change" that so urgently needs to take place and emphasizes that the movement is not just about women, but includes topics such as environmentalism, health care, and LGBTQI rights. Yet, Andary is skeptical as to whether the feminism or the women's march can provide a broader vision for an alternative society and for the future. She admits that numerous single-issue identity political groups have been living in a sort of "bubble", and that this attitude needs to be overcome.

> And that is where intersectionality happens. It is not just about my area, it is not just about women, it is not just about LGBT. It has to be about everything, it has to be that we are fighting and protecting each other, because this is the only way, and this is the thing that scares people. Why do you think so many people downplay the Women's March? It was the first time in history that on the same day it had most people out on the street. (Andary 2018)

In sum, starting with Donald's Trump election and building on the prior mobilizations of movements such as Black Lives Matter, Say Her Name, and Occupy, or the *Precarias de la Deriva* from Spain, the Women's March movement managed to pursue a decidedly intersectional politics. The main focus has been on gender, race and ethnicization, or immigration status. The international dialogue was at first limited to other Women's March chapters abroad and less concerned with dialogue with movements such as *NiUnaMenos* in Latin America.

6.2. #NiUnaMenos

Photo no. 6: TitiNicola. Niunamenos 3J 2018 Santa Fe. June 2018. Wikimedia Commons.

Starting as a protest against femicides and violence against women in 2015, *#NiUnaMenos*/*#NiUnaMás* in Latin America has also grown into one of the largest demonstrations and the most visible feminist movements. The assassination of Chiara Paez in 2016 formed the starting point for the protests, which intensified after the murder of Lucía Pérez in 2017 and the suspicious disappearance of activist Santiago Maldonado. The movements' slogan *Ni una mujer menos, ni una muerte más* (not one woman less, not one more dead/death) also points to feminist predecessors, though from the more recent past: the phrase *Ni Una Muerta Más* (not one dead woman more) was coined in 1995 by the activist and author Susana Chávez to refer to the fight against the femicides in Mexico (Bidaseca 2017, 36). In 2011, Chávez herself was killed. Identifying rhetorically with "all (injured/killed) women", the slogans further embrace a politics of solidarity and joining of forces beyond identity politics that we also see in the context of the Women's March. The contributions to the book make reference to the Women's March, but also to African

American poet and activist Audre Lorde, and Chicana author Cherríe Morraga, who were important precursors of a transnational and intersectional feminist agenda that Karina Bidaseca defines as "a new era of the political/of politics":

> Ni Una Menos in Latin America and the Women's March on Washington are an emblem of a new transnational feminist, anti-racist, anti-imperialist, anti-neoliberal, and anti-heteronormative movement and of the birth of a new era of politics. (Bidaseca and Lois 2017, 10, translation JR)

The dedication to the book *#NiUnaMenos* emphasizes this communal notion of shared embodied experiences and embodied forms of resistance expressed in an inclusive "we":

> Dedicated to the memory of the women who were pulled out of the communities, to the ones who disappeared due to the traffic or the orphaning of their daughters, to the families. They are like every one of us (...) they are not others (...) they are ours, we are them. For a life free of violence against women, for emancipation. We want us alive! (Bidaseca and Lois 2017, 10, translation JR)

María Cecilia Canevari, gender studies researcher and *#NiUnaMenos* organizer at the Universidad de Santiago de Estero in Argentina, admits that there has ultimately been an "explosion" of feminist movements everywhere. However, she emphasizes the importance of keeping in mind that these movements go back to a long trajectory of feminist resistance and organizing. For the current Argentinian contexts, she considers particularly the *Encuentros nacionales de mujeres* national meetings, which have been taking place on an annual basis since 1986, as crucial for the current activism. According to Canevari, who has herself been participating for the last 30 years, these meetings were marked by a very plural participation with intensive debates and the construction of a common agenda: "The encuentros nacionales have been and continue to be a school of feminism" (Canevari 2019, translation JR), she emphasizes. The national campaign for legal, safe, and free abortion emerged from the 2005 national meeting, as well as projects of the *ley en 7 oportu-*

nidades (1995) for equal rights and opportunities, which entered the terrain of the legislative chambers for the first time (ibid.). Besides the legislative claims, the feminist movements in Argentina have worked toward cultural transformations, Canevari underscores. For instance, since the end of the military dictatorship (1979-83), there is a considerable presence of feminists in the academy. And the *ley de cupo femenino* law (1991) guaranteed women access to political representation through quota. Canevari is convinced that the feminist movements pursue a new form of the political, which she considers outwardly difficult in a patriarchal climate and system.

However, she observes that the *#NiUnaMenos* protests represent diversity and other forms of doing politics. "What can we do to feminize politics?" Canevari asks, and she considers the most urgent questions to be: "what shall we do so that our demands reach the center of political debates and no longer remain always marginalized? What do we do to make people understand that the patriarchal and capitalist structures harm our lives, our planet?" (Canevari 2019, translation JR). In order to work towards the demands implicit in these questions, she considers it "important to have anti-systemic practices, be dysfunctional, disturb" (ibid.). To work inside and outside of state and institutional structures and "call to mind that the personal is political, and in every space that we occupy, we can be dysfunctional for the patriarchal order." (ibid.) She considers the mainstream media in Argentina outright *machista*, since the owners are men, and so are the circulating logics. However, in 2018, one of the male-run TV programs put up the debate about legal abortion and offered other perspectives than had previously been broadcasted. Other programs started to address the topic and feminists could be seen on the media – "an unprecedented thing in our country", as Canevari emphasizes. She adds that social media like Facebook, WhatsApp, or Twitter play a very important role for the conservative right as much as for the young feminist movements, and the social movements in general. "The first march of *#NiUnaMenos* on June 3, 2015 was furnished overnight and was multitudinal. This was only possible with social media." (ibid.)

Like the pink "Pussy Hats" that could be seen everywhere during the Women's Marches and for which they have become symbolic, the green bandanas that have become the symbol of the *#NiUnaMenos* demonstrations visually and semiotically unite the different bodies gathering together in protest as a unified "political" body of resistance.

6.2.1. Bodies in Concert: Green Pañuelos

Photo no. 7: TitiNicola. Marcha Ni Una menos en Buenos Aires 40. June 2017. Wikimedia Commons.

First in Argentina and then throughout Latin America, the green *pañuelos* (bandanas and/or headscarves, handkerchiefs) that many *#NiUnaMenos*/*#NiUnaMás* protestors wear, started out as the symbol of the 2018 struggle for the right of access to legal and free abortion. Soon, about eight thousand green bandanas were sold annually for a symbolic price. The bandanas have by now become the symbol of the broader feminist protest (see Muzi 2018, translation JR).

Photo no. 8: ProtoplasmaKid. Green bandanas in Mexico City for legal abortion in Argentina. August 2018. Wikimedia Commons.

The *pañuelos* go back to the tradition of the white headscarves of the mothers and grandmothers of the *Plaza de Mayo* movement in Argentina. These activists demanded explanation for their children's "disappearance" under the military dictatorship through their year-long weekly gatherings and marches and for whom the piece of cloth symbolized diapers which they customized by stitching their children's names on them (and the grandmothers their logo of a dot and a cross).

The first use of the green version by the legal abortion campaigners, according to Carolina Muzi, dates back to 2003 during the *XVIII Encuentro Nacional de Mujeres* in Rosario. These campaigners originally wanted to use a purple bandana, the color historically associated with global feminism, but purple was out of stock. Green was available and the color furthermore had many positive associations, such as hope for a better life for women, as it stands for health (Muzi 2018). In 2018, the number of sales surpassed 200,000. Muzi quotes a fashion designer who argues that the practice of communal dressing is an act of mutual opposition, identification, differentiation and resistance; and she describes this practice as a "disruption of the public space" produced by the green of the bandanas as well as the fact that many protesters also dressed in green or wore green make-up (Muzi 2018). The bandanas are produced by women's co-operatives and can be ordered on the Internet (see the e-commerce platform *Mercado Libre*).

6.2.2. The #Manifiestos

Like the Women's March organizers, the *#NiUnaMenos* protestors soon formulated more concrete political aims, expressed in the form of Manifestos Between June 3, 2015, and March 24, 2019, *#NiUna Menos* published 24 Manifestos on their website, among them manifestos on topics such as *Trabajadoras somos todas* (We are all workers) (Manifiesto #18, May 1, 2018), *Las guerrillas son nuestras compañeras* (the guerilleras are our colleagues/comrades) (Manifiesto #24, March 21, 2019), *El grito en común: ¡Vivas nos queremos!* (the collective cry: We want them alive!) (Manifiesto #3, May 21, 2016*), Ni Una Menos Por Aborto Inseguro* (Not one less due to insecure abortion) (Manifiesto #13, September 25, 2017), or *#DesendeudadasNosQueremos* (We want ourselves debtless) (Manifiesto #11, June 2, 2017) (all from: Resumen Latinoamericano 2019). All the claims made in the manifestos point to an intersectional politics of solidarity and multi-level struggle as well as a holistic and strongly systemic understanding of inequalities and violence as embedded in capitalist economic and colonial power structures and a collective feminist body.

Manifiesto #1 emphasizes the original motivation of the *#Ni UnaMenos* movement, which started out with a focus on violence against women and femicides, but simultaneously already highlighted the systemic character of these assassinations as well as the necessity for collective organizing to scandalize and stop the systematic killings of women for being women:

> In 2008, they killed a woman every 40 hours; in 2014, every 30 hours. In these 7 years, the media published news about 1,808 feminicides. How many women died being murdered for the simple fact of being women? We don't know. But we do know that we have to say stop. In these years, the feminicides made about 1500 girls orphans and forced some of them to live together with the murderers. The problem concerns all of us. The solution must be constructed together. We need to unite commitments in order to change a culture that tends to think of women as consumers and disposable objects and not as autonomous persons. (NiUnaMenos website, translation JR)

Manifiesto #11 underscores the activity of "making body" (*haciendo cuerpo*)as a collective form of protest and opposition to the national debt: "On May 10, we were making/building a collective body on the Plaza de Mayo square to evidence our opposition to the impunity of the crimes of State Terrorism; the government of *Alianza Cambiemos* jeopardized the lives of generations by taking on millions of debt" (Agenda 2019, translation JR). They claim that finance via debts provide a direct form of exploitation of the work force, vital potential and the capacity of organizing women in the home, in the territories. "The machista violence becomes even stronger through the feminization of poverty and the lack of economic autonomy which implies indebtedness." (ibid.) The feminist movement consolidated as a dynamic and transversal social actor, capable of making the diverse forms of economic exploitation visible.

Canevari states that the feminist movement in Argentina is also faced with an increasing "war" against "gender ideology", as can be observed in the documentary produced by CLACAI (*Consorcio Latinoamericano Contra el Aborto Inseguro, Latin American Consortium Against Unsafe Abortion*) titled *Género bajo ataque* (Gender Under Attack). As in many places, in Argentina the growth of the Evangelical Neopentecostal churches is enormous and they are particularly successful in the sectors "impoverished by neoliberal politics and also in the prisons, people with addictions" (Canevari 2019). For Canevari,

> They grow especially where people are suffering, and in the present moment, the economies and the increasing individualization and isolation generate suffering. That is, when everything is bad on earth, religion offers you resignation, comfort, and the promise that at least in the thereafter you will be fine. But the Catholic Church is also fighting. We see a notorious faction against the feminists and the movements for diversity. (ibid.)

In Colombia, for example, church actors have pressured politics to delete all gender-related issues from the constitution after the first referendum (see Duzán 2018). However, as Canevari recounts, her last travels to other Latin American countries have shown her that "the green pañuelos, symbol for the legalization of abortion in Argentina, are known and replicated. We have also seen photos from different cities expressing their solidarity" (Canevari 2019, translation JR). The strikes of March 8 were also significant for the consolidation and internationalization of the movement. Every small city participated in the international strike, "and there is a clear consciousness that we are joining a global movement" (ibid.). Canevari emphasizes the economic and structural dimension of the inequalities this movement addresses and fights, since the Women's strike "allowed a turn of the international Women's Workers' Day that was considered a day of celebration and now it has become clear that it is a commemoration of the struggles of women workers, the ones that died. But it has also made visible the unpaid feminine work that sustains the economy" (ibid.).

In sum, in the US context, the narrative of the recent feminist movements was focused predominantly on uniting different minorities. Like in the above-mentioned publications on the *NiUnaMenos* movement, Canavari puts a stronger emphasis on the importance of the economic dimension and expresses an open critique of capitalism and against violence against women for the protesters in Latin America. In Brazil, the movements following assassination of politician Marielle Franco and the election of right extremist Jair Bolsonaro in 2018 combine both perspectives and furthermore emphasize a strong anti-colonial critique.

6.3. Marielle Presente!, #EleNão and #MulheresContraBolsonaro

Photo no. 9: Yuri Salvador. Marielle, presente! March 2018. Flickr.

In Brazil, the assassination of the openly gay Afro-Brazilian politician Marielle Franco and her driver Anderson Gomes, who were shot with 13 bullets on the night of March 14, 2018, led to massive mobilizations and protests all over the country. Worldwide, more than a million protestors expressed their anger about this brutal murder, which is seen as political by many. As Amnesty International states, there are numerous indicators that point to a professional assassination. According to experts, the ammunition, for instance, stems from the arsenal of the federal police, and the weapons used were registered with the local police. Amnesty International refers to sources from the authorities that indicate that external actors tried to influence the investigation (see Amnesty International 2019). Jurema Werneck, director of Amnesty International Brazil claims in March 2019 that one year after Marielle's death "it is clear that it was a thoroughly planned murder, in which probably also state actors were involved" (ibid.). The authorities that examine Marielle Franco's death have so far neither confirmed nor repudiated whether they are investigating a possible involvement of the military police, local functionaries, militia, or a group of hitmen called "Crime Office", and the investigation of case is marked by numerous unresolved aspects (ibid.).

Marielle Franco was from Maré, one of the biggest *favelas* in the suburbs of Rio de Janeiro and a member and representative of the PSOL party (for socialism and liberty). Marielle was one of the first of her generation to profit from the affirmative action programs put into practice under Lula da Silva. Like only one in 2000 favela inhabitants, she had a university degree. Marielle Franco was also elected as representative of the resistance to the coup d'état against Lula da Silva, and she stood up against inequalities, violence and racism. She continued to live in Maré and became a politician insusceptible to corruption who questioned the privatization of security politics through militia and the neglect of the favelas in favor of tourism and of mega events such as the 2014 FIFA Soccer World Cup or the 2016 Olympics. Politician, activist and former advisor of Marielle Franco Mônica Francisco, in a talk in March 2019 in Berlin, thus described Marielle Franco as someone breaking "with everything normative", since she was representing everything formerly marginalized, and thus was seen as a "threat to order" by conservative and radical right forces (Francisco 2019, translation JR). Francisco sees Marielle's murder as a symbol, because she stood for "all who had no voice in the parliament". From these new – and still very few – positions of visibility, afro-descendants now oppose the "colonialist, extractivist state that discards our bodies" (ibid.). Marielle Franco's death stands in a long tradition of police violence against afro-descendant Brazilians and inhabitants of the poor favela neighborhoods. Francisco sees the current neoliberal and pro-military White supremacist political backlash in Brazil as a "class struggle of a violent elite" and thinks that it is no coincidence that, at the moment Black women enter politics, we see a return of a paramilitary style. Francisco herself joined a commission that examines Bolsonaro's connections with the "paramilitary mafia".

Marielle Franco's assassination was immediately followed by broad protests under the motto "Marielle Presente!" (Marielle [is] present) led by afro-descendant Brazilian women and queers all over Brazil, and soon also in places internationally, among them Berlin, Coimbra, and Lisbon. Marielle's portrait started to adorn walls, streets, and sidewalks in many places in form of posters, graffiti, and stencils. During the 2019 carnival in Rio, the *Estação Primeira de Mangueira*, one of the largest and most successful samba schools in Brazil, which features prominently in the live screening of the carnival, dedicated their performance to Marielle Franco.

An initiative titled Justice for Marielle Franco was signed by famous names as diverse as: Chimamanda Adichie, Ken Loach, Arundhati Roy, Ta-Nehisi Coates, Angela Davis, Jesse Jackson, Edward Snowden, and Noam Chomsky. Columnist Tobias Käufer thus sees Franco as "the face of resistance in Brazil" (Käufer 2019), and Sharrelle Barber claims that the slogan "*Marielle, Presente*!" Becomes a Rallying Cry in the Global Fight Against Racism" (Barber 2018). After Jair Bolsonaro's election to office in October 2018, the protests by afro-descendant feminists and their numerous allies intensified and now provide one of the most active and visible forces of resistance in the increasingly polarizing Brazilian society.

#EleNão and #MulheresContraBolsonaro

In August 2017, Ludmilla Teixeira, a black anarchist born in one of the poorest communities of Salvador, Bahia, created the Facebook page *Mulheres Contra Bolsonaro* (Women United Against Bolsonaro), which accepts only female followers almost 4 million of which have joined the page. Out of this group, a movement under the slogan and hashtag: *#EleNão* – #NotHim emerged, which soon spurred hundreds of thousands of protestors onto the streets of Brazil and around the world, becoming the largest demonstration organized by women in Brazil's history (see Brum 2018). On Twitter, *#EleNão* had more than 193,000 mentions between September 16 and 18, 2018, according to monitoring by researchers at FGV university. Additionally, there were 152 thousand tweets with the hashtag *#Ele Nunca* (#NeverHim). The list of women posting against the far-right candidate includes prominent actresses, journalists and TV presenters. "#EleNão is not just about politics. It is about morals", actress Deborah Secco tweeted to her 3.4 million followers (Uchoa 2018).

By repeating their names and continuously publicly showing their photos on posters, the Black Lives Matter movement and the Say Her Name movement in the US initiated a similar politics of rendering the systemically invisibilized dead bodies of African Americans visible and the structures and actors enabling and committing these murders accountable.

A video posted on the Facebook page of the São Paulo-based citizen movement "*Bancada Ativista*" [Activist Fraction] (Posse Popular de Mandata) [Popular Mandate Property], which is dedicated to elect activists to legislative power. The video starts with "*Marielle Franco presente! Anderson, presente!*" chants by protesters of March 15, 2018, in São Paulo. Posters show slogans such as *Preta LGBTQ Marielle Presente* (Black LGBTQ Marielle Present), *Vidas negras e faveladas importam* (Black and Favela Lives Matter) carried by a young Black girl, or *Somos Todxs Marielle* (We are all Marielle). An interviewee (Bianca) states "Marielle está presente en cada uma de nós" (Marielle is present in every one of us). By claiming Marielle Franco's presence in everything she stood for – a Black lesbian woman from the favela who had reached a high position in politics and fought for social justice – and simultaneously claiming to be Marielle Franco ("we are all Marielle"), the predominantly Black female and queer protesters, who are joined by allies of all positions, also unite their precarious bodies in the streets. In doing so, they politically, symbolically, and discursively form a collective body of resistance to the violent racist, sexist, misogynist, and homophobic political climate they face, practicing a politics of embodied intersectionality from below. Marielle Franco has turned into a symbol of this intersectional struggle:

> Marielle Franco will stand as a symbol of the emergent struggles over Brazil's future. Some mourners now find comfort in the hope that her assassination will be a turning point in a wider rejection of the militarization of public security under the current government. But the fierce opposition to Franco as an advocate for marginalized peoples—Afro-Brazilians, women, LGTBQI people, favela residents—illustrates both the force of her message as well as the lengths some will go to silence it. (Cardoso and Ystanes 2018)

At the same time, the number of women and LGBTQI persons in the Brazilian parliament reached a historic low point, as Maya Salam (2018) observes: "(o)f the 964 candidates this year, 272 are women, 215 are people of color and 26 are openly L.G.B.T.Q. The share of candidates who are white men – 58 percent – is the lowest of the last four elections" (Salam 2018). However, as Francisco concludes, "we now make politics, our presence signifies that this process is irreversible" (Francisco 2019, translation JR). For the aim of gaining a voice and imagining politics otherwise, she sees Black feminism as important, since Black feminism is inclusive and builds important strategic alliances. Moreover, it functions as a collective, circular form without being "polite" (ibid.).

By claiming "Marielle's presence" and her political legacy alive as well as demanding her murder to be clarified, spraying her portrait as graffiti on walls in public spaces and on posters in the streets, the protestors resist a politics that invisibilizes and marginalizes murders motivated by racist, sexist, and homo and transphobic motives (see the memorial site for Marielle Franco: www.mariellefranco.com.br.). "We have begun to destroy the myth of equality," she continues, since due to their history, afro-descendant Brazilians "are resistant, rebellious bodies" (Francisco 2019). Sharrelle Barber, who had attended the event Marielle Franco joined the night before her assassination, is convinced that Marielle Franco was assassinated both for speaking for Blacks and the poor in the favelas and against police brutality, and because she had just been elected to a powerful position with the fifth highest vote count out of 51 city councilors voted into local office in Rio. Barber is sure the protest following her death – which she notably imagines as "an army of Marielles" and thus also a (strategically) united body in struggle – will help to continue her political legacy and the resistance to racist, homophobic, and sexist right-wing forces:

> The mass protests following her death and the images of black women leading the charge (…) assured me that indeed the resistance is alive and well, her legacy will live on and an army of Marielles – strong, bold, brilliant, unflinching black women – will and must rise and take her place. Indeed, Marielle Presente. (Barber 2018)

*

All of the mentioned protests started out as spontaneous and momentous events based on very diverse politics. With the International Women's Strike starting on March 8, 2016, the different movements have become more organized and politically more concrete and focused, raising hope for a more institutionalized and long-lasting way of contestation.

7. From the Protest Marches to the 8 M Women's International Strike

The International Women's Strike, also known as *Paro Internacional de Mujeres*, coincided with International Women's Day, on 8 March 2017 and 2018. As of 2020, the Strike has become a global movement coordinated across over 50 countries. The idea of a women's strike gets back to a 1975 protest in Iceland. On March 8, 2000, the *Campaña Internacional por un Salario para el Trabajo en el Hogar* called the first International Women's Strike, demanding the women's right to justice for their unrecognized contribution to the workforce. The movement was especially active during the years 2000-2001. On October 19, 2016, in Argentina, members of the movement *Ni Una Menos* and other feminist organizations, like the Spanish *Internacional Feminista*, called for an hour-long strike and various demonstrations, after a week with 7 femicides. The first Women's March on Washington was also held on January 21, 2017. The first International Women's Strike was on March 8, 2017, and took place in more than 50 countries around the world. Protests such as the International Day for the Elimination of Violence against Women on November 25, 2017 in different countries, and the massive answer to the call of the Women's March 2018 in the United States are considered as precedents. During the third ITUC World Women's Conference/Women's Organizing Assembly in October 2017, 200 female trade unionists gathered from around the world in Costa Rica, and trade unionist representatives from Argentina and Brazil asked the unions to take part in the second International Women's Strike call on March 8, 2017.

Under slogans like #*NosParamos*, #WeStrike, and "What they call love is unpaid work", the feminist movements called for a strike from workers, students, care workers and consumers. One of the main demands was for a society free from violence against women, whose most visible manifestation is the aggression and murder of women for the simple fact of being women. Women's labor rights were also defended, affected by precarious work, the gender pay gap and sexual harassment in the workplace. Poverty, racial violence, persecution of immigrants and cutbacks in social and health programs were also reported. A flyer for the March 8 strike in Argentina emphasized the harsh opposition to the current politics, but also the structural oppression these politics build on: *Si nuestras vidas no valen, ¡produzcan sin nosotras!* – if our lives don't count, produce without us! – thereby hinting at the economic structures that are based on the unequal, racialized and gendered division of labor and the precarity and often disposability of certain bodies (Bidaseca and Lois 2017, 9).

The strikes are significant for at least two reasons: first, they happened in many places around the globe, meaning they are transnational and second, they seemingly concentrated and articulated claims and politics previously expressed by many separate movements and related them to the global and structural level of capitalist racialized and gendered exploitation and oppression.

> In the two Women's Strikes we organized in less than one year, together with women's unionists and other organizations of all sorts, we were able to put on the agenda and assemble demands of formal labor and of the unemployed, of the popular economies together with the historical vindication of recognition of the unpaid labor that we women carried out, and to politicize care and the recognition of self-employed labor. Within this framework, we believe it is necessary to advance in addressing the renewed forms of exploitation that impoverish our living conditions and make our existences precarious, that build the frame in which the number of femicides has doubled. These are numbers that are in intimate relation. (ibid.)

In the United States, inspired by calls from Argentina and other Latin American countries, the Women's march organizers also joined the Women's Strike on March 8, 2017, two weeks after the first 2017 March (WMO 2018, 253). Alyssa Klein retrospectively sees the Day Without A Woman as "a test for the Women's March, a test of whether we could keep it up and this wasn't just a one-shot event that was going to be over in a few months" (Klein, WMO 2018, 253). The organizers received a lot of protest for the decision to join the strike. Women's March organizer Cassady Fendlay confirms that they were harshly criticized by people who saw them as too radical and accused them of distracting the focus from women's rights (Fendlay 2019). She admits that in the US, "many people are not aware what's going on elsewhere." She underscores, however, that the idea to call the US versions of the strike "A Day Without A Woman" is closely related to the experiences of Latina women of colonialism and racism, who had protested their work conditions under the motto "A Day Without a Mexican" and "A Day Without an Immigrant". For Fendlay, the participation in the strike provided a decisive step towards establishing more sustainable structures:

> I think it was a really big deal to be putting this radical messaging out there. The power of the people to collectively strike and withdraw their labor from the system for a day was really rocking the boat. I hope that it laid a lot of groundwork, especially for young people who will see this as something viable, a power-building tactic. (Fendlay, WMO 2018, 253)

The scope of the Women's strikes also becomes visible in the call for a strike published in The Guardian on February 6, 2017, by prominent activists and intellectuals Linda Martín Alcoff, Cinzia Arruzza, Tithi Bhattacharya, Nancy Fraser, Barbara Ransby, Keeanga-Yamahtta Taylor, Rasmea Yousef Odeh, and Angela Davis (Alcoff et al. 2018). The initiators explicitly mention the impact of the Latin American, particularly the Argentinian, movements with regard to intersectional politics, addressing structural problems and coalition building:

> We take inspiration from the Argentinian coalition Ni Una Menos. Violence against women, as they define it, has many facets: it is domestic violence, but also the violence of the market, of debt, of capitalist property relations, and of the state; the violence of discriminatory policies against lesbian, trans and queer women; the violence of state criminalization of migratory movements; the violence of mass incarceration; and the institutional violence against women's bodies through abortion bans and lack of access to free

> healthcare and free abortion. (…) Let us join together on 8 March to strike, walk out, march and demonstrate. Let us use the occasion of this international day of action to be done with lean-in feminism and to build in its place a feminism for the 99%, a grassroots, anti-capitalist feminism – a feminism in solidarity with working women, their families and their allies throughout the world. (Alcoff et al. 2018)

The authors emphasize that they think the march was not enough and that the "attack on women", which in their view long predates Trump's administration, needs more than a spontaneous opposition to Trump's "aggressively misogynistic, homophobic, transphobic and racist policies". Here, like the Latin American activists by whom they feel inspired, they accentuate the systemic dimension of the oppressions and inequalities they address: "Rather it needs to target the ongoing neoliberal attack on social provision and labor rights." (ibid) Echoing the notion of the "99%" that had become famous during the Occupy movement, the authors ask for a "feminism of the 99%" that they already see "emerging internationally", and situate their struggle in this tradition: "from the women's strike in Poland against the abortion ban to the women's strikes and marches in Latin America against male violence; from the vast women's demonstration of last November in Italy to the protests and the women's strike in defense of reproductive rights in South Korea and Ireland" (ibid.). Underscoring the combined struggles these feminist movements mobilize, the authors thus call for an expanded agenda that is "at once anti-racist, anti-imperialist, anti-heterosexist and anti-neoliberal" (ibid.). In order to contribute to this new feminist movement, they propose as a first step to join the other 30 countries and build an international strike against male violence and reproductive rights on March 8. As these US American activists mention, the attention to the structural dimensions of oppression and the urgency of the entanglements with global capitalism and the division of labor that the authors call for had already been a central task in parts of the Latin American feminist movements.

In February 2019, a similar call and manifesto for the "general and international" women's strike titled *Llamamiento al paro feminista 8M 2019* (Call for Feminist Strike 8 March 2019) was published in a national newspaper and on various online platforms by the organizers of the *Ni Una Menos* collective in Argentina a month ahead of the 8 March 2019 Women's strikes and demonstrations. This text is also based on a decidedly intersectional understanding of "feminist" struggle, pursuing a clear-cut critique of global neoliberal capitalism. In the election year in Argentina, the text seeks to unite a number of battles based on the structural exploitation and oppression of women and differently gendered persons as well as precarious and marginalized groups across borders (Llamamiento al paro feminista 8M 2019, see Resumen Latinoamericano 2019):

> This year we organize the feminist strike all over the world. We all go on strike: in the households, in the markets, in the factories, in the universities, and in all working spaces; in the forest, in the occupied territories and in the slums; in the popular economies and the precarious works; in the streets and in the communities, and in the hospitals and in the countryside. We go on strike all over the place and broaden the strike once more: let's make their borders explode, let's invent new geographies. Let's thereby redefine the very spaces where work is being done and value is being produced. Let's recognize and dignify the historically invisibilized and devaluated forms of labor: reproductive work, communitarian work, migrant work. (Resumen Latinoamericano 2019, translation JR)

Particular emphasis is put on the structural inequalities inscribed in the gendered and international division of labor and the devaluation of reproductive and care work. The movement is motivated by the resulting violence against women and differently gendered people of all sorts, ranging from domestic violence to the illegalization of abortion and feminicide:

> We also strike against the heteropatriarchal family and domestic confinement, against the exploitation of our territories, against the sexual abuse by the machos in positions of power, against the femi-

> cides and travesticides, against the criminalization of migrants, against the clandestineness of abortion, against patriarchal justice, against the systematic impoverishment and indebtedness, against the assassination of territorial leaders, against racism, against religious fanaticisms, and the moralization of our desires. Because we go on strike against the structures and mandates that make the valorization of capital possible. (ibid.)

The manifesto read during the strike strongly denunciated the economic crisis, the cuts in health and education expenditures, and the suspension of staff under the Macri government in Argentina. The protest also confronted the influence of the Catholic Church and called for the implementation of "secular integral sexual education" based on scientific, feminist and gender studies perspectives as well as transgender and disability rights, and the integration of afro-indigenous women.

By physically assembling on the streets, these women and their allies took a stand against the historic and continuous control, precarity and disposability of female and differently gendered and racialized as well as poor and colonized bodies. Gabriela Lozano Rubella points out how the activities around the strike of March 8, 2019, brought together artists and academic camps and managed to organize an impressive mobilization of different forces:

> Between the more than 100,000 persons that assembled in the mobilization to the Plaza de Mayo Square there were women, lesbians, transvestites, transpersons, bisexuals, non-binary people, fat and intersex persons from the working class. On the horizon, besides the diversity, the dominion of the color green was evident. The bandanas de Campaña Nacional por el Aborto Legal, Seguro y Gratuito [campaign for legal, safe and free abortion] surrounded the puppets, the arms and heads of the young and adult women, they decorated purses and backpacks, other women covered their breasts with them. (Lozano Rubello 2019, translation JR)

Various contributors to the 8 M book make reference to Rosa Luxemburg's notion of strike as "path and process" and critical practice (e.g. Gago 2018, 18-19). Based on the experience of the "precarity of existence as communal condition" (ibid. 13, translation JR), Gago sees the strike as an opportunity for "other ways of thinking the territory and particularly the body as territory (body-territory)" (ibid.). Resonating with Silvia Federici's notion of the female body as equivalent to the factory for wageworkers in capitalist systems, and thus the main territory of exploitation and resistance in the protests and strikes, their bodies rise and resist their exploitation and the unequal structures built on it (Federici, cf. in Draper 2018, 71).

*

As we have seen, the current feminist movements address multidimensional and intersectional axes of oppression and relate them to the structural inequalities like patriarchy, neoliberal capitalism and colonial legacies that reproduce them. In all of the recent movements, manifold precarious bodies unite, contest, protest, and resist the colonial violence and the resulting persistent and revived inequalities and claim a new form of the political, a new language:

> Is it possible that we are building a new language that allows us to dispute the sense/feelings involved in the violence against women? (...) it's a new language that invites us to put our bodies, to stand up everyday for what we believe. It's not about media acts that multiply a slogan, but about understanding that we all constitute a patriarchal society that pigeonholes us, that injects us a conscience and pre-established roles, and marks the norms of how social relations "must be". (Vacca 2017, 41, translation JR)

By bringing together diverse and manifold precarious bodies and bodies in solidarity in the streets and in networks to oppose racists and sexist right-wing attacks, the current feminist movements oppose, contest, and resist the right-wing populist ethnosexism we currently encounter everywhere. In theory and through their practices, these movements simultaneously elaborate on the concept of intersectionality by recognizing the inequalities as structural ones that are deeply embedded in the capitalist system and in a long history of racist-colonial and en-gendered oppression. All the examples of feminist contestation discussed above demonstrate that the movements in both parts of the hemisphere go beyond classical feminist "single issue" struggles. In fact, these new feminist movements see themselves as alliances of solidarity that collectively denounce different groups and different axes of inequality and entangled forms of oppression towards alternative notions of sociability. Isabell Lorey thus provides an outward euphoric outlook on the potential of the movements as a new form of the political:

> The transnational feminist strike wave is directed against racism, against closed borders and exclusive nationalisms, against military, extreme-rightwing and populist masculinisms, against the exploitative relations of neoliberal capitalism and against the 'anti-genderism' promoted not least by the Vatican and the Catholic Church. These are giant demonstrations in which millions participate, and which are unfolding a monstrous new feminist and queer power worldwide, a forceful wave that can overflow everything. (Lorey 2019b)

Elaborating on the particularities and the potential of the current feminist movements, Susana Draper focuses on the new articulations the current feminist activism brings about, which she speaks of as a "poetics" of solidarity and intersectionality, which she observes in the posters and the speeches at the marches. The silenced gender and all its allies sing, chant, and dance, and thus claims a space and visibility in the very space it had historically been banned from. Creative and artistic forms play a pivotal role here, as many such contributions at the Women's Marches, *#NiUnaMenos* demonstrations and the 8 M Strikes illustrate. Referring back to a long memory of resistance to which Black and decolonial anti-capitalist feminists like Angela Davis and Silvia Federici connect the current movements, she ascribes this language the potential of being "a poetics of struggle toward a new feminism" (una poética de lucha hacia un Nuevo feminismo, Draper 2018, 64). Draper underscores the new articulations of processes hitherto restricted to the academy that the movements until 8 M have re-connected with actual struggles (65). She wonders how the anti-capitalist potential of the "key word" of intersectionality as an analysis of "interlocking oppressions and the workings of power can be re-articulated, appropriated and re-signified" (67).

8. Outlook Part II: A New Poetics of Solidarity and Intersectionality?

The currently emerging feminist struggles are embedded in the radicalization of reactionary White heteronormative masculinism in many places and contexts that currently seeks to oppose the pluralization of societies and life forms expressed in right-wing populism, as elaborated on in the first part of this study. In *Notes Toward a Performative Theory of Assembly* (2015), Judith Butler describes the current moment as "a biopolitical situation" in which diverse populations are increasingly affected by so-called "precarization". As she argues, this precarization becomes operative through the overall pulverization of the active remnants of social democracy, while promoting ideologies of individual responsibility according to which subjects are obliged to constantly maximize their market value in an entrepreneurial way and see this as the ultimate goal (15). In turn, pursuing the question of what function public assembly can serve in this context, what "opposing form of ethics" it embodies and expresses, she concludes that, amidst "an increasingly individualized sense of anxiety and failure", public assembly "embodies the insight that this social condition is both shared and unjust", hence "assembly enacts a provisional and plural form of coexistence that constitutes a distinct ethical and social alternative to 'responsibilization.'" (15-16).

Through the dialogue between diverse histories and notions of the political there emerges what Gago terms the "precipitate subject" (sujeto imprevisto; Gago 2018, 22) of feminism. Through the "corporal rootage" (arraign corporal) this subject evokes the (for many: colonial) wound as condition for dislocating the political scene (Gago 2018, 22-23). The creation of the communal body of feminist resistance enables the thinking and imagining of a new poetics and new figures of connectivity and dialogue between "Norths and Souths" (conectividad entre nortes y sures, Draper 2018, 65). Butler also speaks about the importance of "embodied" forms of resistance. Feminists of Color and post- and decolonial feminists like

Alanna Lockward – who curated the series "BE.BoP – Black Europe Body politics" foregrounding performative form of decolonial aesthtetics (Lockward 2013) – or Grada Kilomba – "the body as political tool" (Kilomba 2019) – have long emphasized a similar notion of the body. They have particularly emphasized its potential for using the "knowledges of the body" to attack the "colonial-anti-capitalist unconscious" and politically "become one body" (Bardet 2018, 110, translation JR). Maria Lugones (2010) respectively speaks of "resistant subjectivities" embodied by colonized women who are constantly trying to deny oppression. Persons racialized as Black in the context of colonization and enslavement have historically been denied the same status of a body as Whites and been reduced to the status of "pure flesh", as Hortense Spillers has shown. According to Butler (2015), the very presence of these bodies in public proclaims the fact that they are not disposable, "they are exercising a plural and performative right to appear, one that asserts and instates the body in the middle of the political field" (11) and thus, orchestrate a "plural and embodied performativity (…) marked by dependency and resistance" (18). Acting in concert, then, "can be an embodied form of calling into question the inchoate and powerful dimensions of reigning notions of the political" (9).

By promoting, defending, and, most of all, embodying diversity, the present movements make visible and open up the possibility for alternative forms of the social and political in light of neoliberal precarization and right-wing populist "responses" or "answers". By their very presence and claims, they call into question the "repressive dogma that has cast so many genders and sexual lives into the shadows, without recognition and deprived of any sense of futurity" (Butler 2019) – and are therefore hated and feared by their right-wing and conservative opponents. The Women's Strikes in particular provide an important arena for feminists claims and for countering the neoliberal and right-wing trends, as they call attention to the notion of violence against women as a structural phenomenon and the structural devaluation of care work and reproduction as well as socio-political power relations of discrimination, exclusion and deportation. They thus provide a means to understand the current movements and alliances always as transversal and intersectional. The strikes provide a transnational instrument open to a multitude of actors, not only for women, but also for precarious and migrant workers (see Lorey 2019).

As the numerous references to (mostly Women of Color) predecessors demonstrate, the protestors situate their struggles in this tradition. Thereby, a new sense of intersectionality is being evoked that re-connects the concept with the radical activist and practical roots it emerged from after it had long been restricted to academic and theoretical debates. According to Butler, the "bodies in alliance" (2015, 28) making their protest and claims visible in the streets of Washington, Buenos Aires, Rio de Janeiro, Berlin, New York, Warsaw and many other places, point to the social modality of bodies and "link gender and sexual minorities with precarious populations more generally" (ibid.). By performing a political unity based on manifold positions and experiences – as expressed in the emblematic Pink Pussy hats of the Women's Marches, the green bandanas of the *Ni Una Menos* movement, or the graffiti of and identification with Marielle Franco in Brazil – the protesters also make visible and audible the "conditions of interdependency" (45 and 50) of all human interaction and sociability as well as a politics of intersectionality restored into practice, in the form of a particular "embodied intersectionality" (Mirza 2013).

Part III

9. Outlook

The current wave of right-wing populist actors represents a renewed struggle over cultural and political hegemony in the context of intensifying inequalities and increasing social precarization and insecurity. In this climate, hegemonic strands of feminism are perceived as being co-opted by and/or representative of the neoliberal values of individualism, economization of social relations, and competitiveness. These strands, which go back to the liberal claims for equal rights and individual freedom, clearly did not speak out loud enough – or simply were not aware of – their slinking incorporation into neoliberal politics linked to a struggle over resources and the related defamation of feminism(s) or its loss of impact through consumerist versions.

Right-wing populist actors use – or, rather, emerge from and are fed by – current insecurities in order to mobilize against emancipatory and liberal achievements. Gender serves them as an arena and meta-language for modulating and re-ordering social constellations. As the exemplary cases from the US and Brazil have demonstrated, gender is used in various, shifting and context-specific ways to achieve this aim. Due to the systematic affinities of media with populism, mass media, and, increasingly, social media, populist actors are able to mobilize emotions and affects – a pattern I have termed "fake news and/or affective truths". Gender topics are a specifically valuable field for this goal of creating hegemony, since gender is incorporated into "chains of equivalence" (Laclau 2005, 84) between different requests, turning them into demands or into an "empty signifier" to "name all wrongs". Gender appeals to the everyday experiences of all people and moreover is already based on a binary and hierarchical naturalized structure. Since this structure is embodied by many, it can easily be evoked to create "affective truths", such as the notion that women are affectively responsible for care work. Gender thus also meets the media logic of the need for simplicity of arguments and creating scandals – often sex scandals that are mostly related to the female body – in tune with the attention economy typical for mass media. The disregard of taboo and the effectiveness of scandals are also at the heart of the phenomenon that we particularly observe in the US and Brazil, where both presidents have been accused of sexist and racist assaults. Even though both have occasionally strategically withdrawn from their statements, they worked to do away with the "political correctness" imposed by the liberal (and perceived as "corrupt and left-wing") elites and toward the expansion of what may be said.

Further, the interpellation of traditional masculinist patterns has served the re-masculinization of politics – significantly after both countries faced the first non-white and working-class presidents and female presidential candidates in history. I have termed this pattern "(White) Re-Masculinization: "Genderism" as Existential Threat." This again also attracted numerous female voters and supporters who felt either attacked in their lifestyles or hoped to gain through femonational alliances with men and, mostly, against immigrants, Muslims, feminists and LGBTQI activists or other minorities. In the employed imaginary, immigrants are constructed as an existential threat, as a menace to "autochthonous" women and a threat to the (reproduction) of the nation. I call the respective patterns "Appropriating Women's Rights" (and the related en-gendering "Femonationalist Alliances") and "Ethno-sexism and Exclusive Intersectionality". Through the related ethno-sexist outsourcing of sexism to the immigrant (often Muslim) Other, the appropriate more emancipated and superior sexual and gender regime can be claimed, while simultaneously ethnically engendering social inequalities and fear. Paradoxically, however, the sexual freedom of women (and, partly, even gays) promoted by right-wing populists is usually restricted to certain women: women who represent the "real people" and support their politics and who are not "feminists". Through the inclusion of certain women's rights, the fight against "genderism" allows right-wing populists to perform a sort of modernization – which in the current social climate of diversification and pluralization often appears to have become necessary, if not inevitable.

Simultaneously, however, these groups are reviving and (re-) naturalizing traditional gender roles and hierarchies. That is also why "gender ideology" is frequently cast as one of the most pressing threats to right-wing conceptions of the "normal" (heteronormative and nuclear) family and the (real) "people" and its "natural" reproduction. The extreme right-wing and often religiously-influenced campaign against "gender ideology as ideological colonization" – which is also the name of my related pattern – further enables the construction of this menace as a global threat against which it constructs an alliance of right-wing and conservative religious players from various faiths. Through this pattern of what I have termed "reverse anti-colonialism", right-wing actors can position their own group as victims and as a "minority" under attack.

Through all these patterns – which occasionally combine and overlap, but also contradict each other – gender thus serves right-wing populists as a tool or affective bridge (Dietze 2019) for catapulting diverse topics into the public sphere, ranging from questions of demography and immigration to border regimes and belonging, to education, the division of labor, resource distribution and social welfare. Against this backdrop, this study has argued that an intersectional – mostly racialized and structurally colonial – gender dimension was no side effect, but was foundational and formative for all social, cultural, economic and political processes in the Americas. The observed contradictions provide right-wing populist actors a sort of epistemic arena in which to re-negotiate what is perceived as common sense and to create a parallel reality which has to be defended against its internal and external enemies, all of whom are discursively framed through gender. Thereby, gender serves to justify the maintenance of traditional gender orders based on male privilege, White supremacy and a particular en-gendered division of labor and reproduction – often while pretending to follow a modernization paradigm which femonational and femoglobal alliances help to put forward. The contestations to women's and LGBTQI's rights can thus be performed as a form of self-defense. These often paradox phenomena require new responses. As Dietze (2018) argues, by using gender politics – such as programmatic gender-conservatism and simultaneous female leadership and the claim that women are already emancipated – right-wing populism creates a dynamic paradox. That is, the inherent contradictions of such politics are not resolved, but remain in movement and are constantly negotiated anew, working with simultaneities and "as well as" and "either"/"or" thereby creating a new style of politics, working through affirmations.

*

As the current feminist movements that have been the focus of the second part of the study indicate, gender and anti-sexism also build a platform for a contestation to the contestation by the right-wing actors to women's and LGBTQI rights. The politics of anti-genderism elaborated on in the first part of this study severely limit rights and diversity and the freedom of choice. Like many of their Pan-American predecessors, the activists of the Women's March, *#Ni UnaMenos*, *#NiUnaMas*, and *Marielle Presente!* movements place the myth of separateness, pureness, and linearity that populists pursue – which often also goes unquestioned in hegemonic feminist discourses – under severe scrutiny. By building a strategic imagined (counter-)community as formulated by America Ferrera in her speech at the 2017 Women's March in Washington, current intersectional transnational and transversal feminists raise the hope for an effective counter-discourse to the current rise and revival of White supremacist and racist, sexist and homo- and transphobic right-wing populism internationally. The feminist movements practice what I – even before discovering that Mirza (2013) had already used the same term – have termed "embodied intersectionality" to confront and stop the right-wing trend. First, feminist protestors unite different bodies that are precarious and invisibilized and politically voiceless through masculinist, nativist White supremacist discourse in the public space, making their presences a "claim" (Butler 2015). Evoking a long legacy of colonial-racist and patriarchal oppression, many of the protesters thus uncover the structures that make unchecked White male public speaking possible to begin with. This happened exactly through the oppression of the colonized and of colonized women, through the silencing and restriction of the female to the domestic and the imaginary of the female body as territory (Federici). This becomes evident in the movements' intersectional and inclusive scope, the explicit aim of coalition building and addressing of structural dimensions of inequalities. Moreover, the current movements seek to render problematic and overcome (some) feminism(s)' complicity with neoliberal logics (which, as we have seen, can sometimes also be co-opted by populist forces). The long legacy of anti-racist feminist struggles in the Americas in particular offers the current movements a rich repertoire of experiences and resistance strategies to counter the right-wing populist and extremist trend.

The strategic political alliances that can – so far – be observed in feminist movements such as the Women's Marches and *Ni Una Menos*, indicate a transcendence of the narrow focus on identity, diversity, and plurality or single-issue struggles of prior phases. Such new forms of solidarity also challenge the tendency to prioritize identity and find individual solutions for structural problems. This tendency could also be observed in significant parts of feminist, postcolonial, and cultural studies approaches. Further studies will have to connect these observations to a more systematic analysis of right-wing populism and gender and relate them to concrete case studies.

*

As my primary observations indicate, an intersectional gender perspective and an intersectional reading can provide decisive new insights to the research and theorizing on right-wing populism in the context of the current crises with regards to aspects of its discursive functioning and logics that are otherwise invisible. An intersectional gender lens can, on the one hand, help to better analyze, describe and criticize current right-wing populist tendencies and the related racist, sexist and homophobic politics. On the other hand, an intersectional gender approach can offer new points of entry for new conceptualizations and theoretical frameworks for the current climate of struggles over hegemony. A respective radical, intersectional, relational feminist approach can help to bring the multiple positioned workings of feminisms and the corresponding alliances into view. Such a perspective widens the scope toward thinking through new analytical categories and spatialities in the Americas based on solidarity and connectedness, and also works towards critically rethinking and overcoming the division between theory and practice, movements/activism and the academy.

It might however be a little too early to celebrate the success of the new feminisms, despite their impressive outreach. On the one hand, there has so far been little active interaction between different feminist movements in the Americas (e.g. between Women's March and the *Ni una menos* Movements, the latter of which started prior to the Women's March in Mexico and Argentina.) Furthermore, time will tell how sustainable the movements will be and whether more transnational alliances will emerge in the future. Also, it remains to be seen how successful the institutionalization and impact of the different movements will be in the long run and with regard to altering the structural level. First and foremost, however, it is yet unpredictable how successful the movements can be in light of the current climate of alternative truths and realities, which prevent the emergence of real agonisms – which Mouffe (in contrast to antagonisms) considers to be the prerequisites for democracy (Mouffe 2018, 106). Strategies like the complete defamation of constructed "enemies" or of self-victimization through what I termed "reverse anti-colonialism", create new paradigms, the language and tools for which still need to be invented. The described movements create hope that the necessary counter-strategies are at least in the making.

10. Acknowledgements

I thank all those who have made this study possible and have accompanied me in the process of researching and writing it – even though this text can only be the start for much more extended and profound research. My deepest gratitude goes to Gabriele Dietze for inspiring me to focus on the topic to begin with and for our ongoing stimulating dialogues, discussions, and projects. Our workshop "Right-Wing Populism and Gender" at the ZiF in Bielefeld in November 2018 was crucial for the way the text educed. I am also thankful to Eleonora Rohland for hosting the very first roundtable on populism with me, to Paula Diehl for participating and for her continuous input on populism, as well as to Birgit Sauer for insisting on the necessity of a gender perspective in populism research. I am further grateful to all the activists I had the opportunity to speak to, namely Cassady Fendlay (thanks to Katharina Pühl for making the first connection!), Sofia Andary, Monica Franciso and María Cecilia Canevari. Moreover, I am grateful for the opportunity to present parts of this study at the Instituto Colombo-Alemán para la Paz (CAPAZ) in Bogotá and particularly for the helpful comments by Mara Viveros Vigoya who continues to be a great source of inspiration. I am also thankful to Isabel Caldeira for the opportunity to present at the Centro dos Estudos Socais at the Universidade de Coimbra, the DGfA conference in Hamburg (thanks to Simon Schleusener and Simon Strick), the British-German Dialogue on Gender and Populism hosted by the Friedrich-Ebert Foundation and to Shermin Langhoff for the invitation to present a panel at the "Herbstsalon" of the Maxim-Gorki Theater on "De-Heimatize Belonging" in Berlin.

Many thanks also to the wonderful CIAS team at Bielefeld University, particularly, Olaf Kaltmeier, Wilfried Raussert, Albert Manke, and Eleonora Rohland, as well as the Gender Studies crew, Heidemarie Winkel, Alexandra Scheele and Tomke König for ongoing valuable input and dialogue. Special thanks go to the BMBF project "The Americas as Space of Entanglements" for the support and to Edith Otero Quezada for the diligent help with the manuscript and images. I am thankful to my friends and family (chosen, Flamenco, and other) for keeping me save and sane no matter the hardships, and I owe gratitude to Thomas Krüger, my favorite dancer and brother in crime for his relentless positive energy and inspiration. I dedicate this book to my adorable niece Polly Luz Roth, the next generation.

11. Works Cited

Abi-Hassan, Sahar. 2017. “Populism and Gender.” In *The Oxford Handbook on Populism*, ed. Cristóbal Rovira Kaltwasser, Paul Taggart, Paulina Ochoa Espejo and Pierre Ostiguy, 2-22. Oxford: Oxford University Press.

Ahmed, Sara. 2010. *The Promise of Happiness*. Durham, NC.: Duke University Press.

Ajanovic, Edma, Stefanie Mayer and Birgit Sauer. 2018. “Constructing ‘the people’: An intersectional analysis of right-wing concepts of democracy and citizenship in Austria.” *Journal of Language and Politics* 17, no. 5, 636-654.

Al-Asawiya, Aisha Sister, 2018. “Sankofa: Look Back to Move Forward.” In *Together We Rise: The Women’s March. Behind the Scenes at the Protest Heard around the World*, ed. The Women’s March Organizers and Condé Nast, 73-74. New York: HarperCollins.

Alcoff, Linda et al. 2018. “We need a feminism for the 99%. That’s why women will strike this year.” *The Guardian* online edition, January 27.

Amnesty International. 2019. “Ein Jahr nach Mord an Marielle Franco: Behörden müssen Verantwortliche vor Gericht stellen.” https://www.amnesty.de/informieren/aktuell/brasilien-ein-jahr-nach-mord-marielle-franco-behoerden-muessen-verantwortliche.

Andary, Sofia. 2018. Interview by Julia Roth. San Francisco, April 18.

Assheuer, Thomas. 2018. “Kitsch und Kampf.” *Die Zeit* online edition, July 26.

Bancada Activista. 2018. “Marielle, presente!” https://www.facebook.com/bancadaativista/videos/1965805397071043/.

Barber, Sharrelle. 2018. “‘Marielle, Presente!’ Becomes a Rallying Cry in the Global Fight Against Racism.” *Sojourners*. https://sojo.net/articles/marielle-presente-becomes-rallying-cry-global-fight-against-racism.

Bardet, Marie. 2018. "Excursus. ¿Cómo hacemos un cuerpo?" In *8M: Constelación Feminista. ¿Cuál es tu Huelga? ¿Cuál es tu Lucha?*, ed. Verónica Gago et al., 109-113. Buenos Aires: Tinta Limón.

Bashi Treitler, Vilna. 2013. *The Ethnic Project. Transforming Racial Fiction into Ethnic Factions*. Stanford: Stanford University Press.

Bassimir, Anja-Maria. 2018. "Definition – Macht – Evangelikal: Standortbestimmung zum gegenwärtigen U.S.-amerikanischen Evangelikalismus." *Amerikastudien / American Studies* 63, no. 3, 389-422.

Belausteguigoitia, Marisa. 2009. *Güeras y prietas. Género y raza en la construcción de mundos nuevos*. México City: UNAM.

Bidaseca, Karina. 2017. "81800 muertas por feminicidio, 700 desaparecidas y más." In *#NiUnaMenos. Vivxs nos queremos*, 35-37. Buenos Aires: Milena Caserola.

Bidaseca, Karina and Ianina Lois. 2017. "8M: Ni una Menos: Paro Internacional de Mujeres." In *#NiUnaMenos. Vivxs nos queremos*, 9-14. Buenos Aires: Milena Caserola.

Boatcă, Manuela. 2015. *Global Inequalities Beyond Occidentalism*. Farnham: Ashgate.

Boatcă, Manuela and Julia Roth. 2016. "Unequal and Gendered: Notes on the Coloniality of Citizenship Rights." *Current Sociology* 64, no. 2, 191-212.

Boatcă, Manuela and Julia Roth. 2019. "Women on the Fast Track? Coloniality of Citizenship and Embodied Social Mobility." In *Gender and Development: The Economic Basis of Women's Power*, ed. Samuel Con and Rae L. Blumberg, 162-174. London: Sage Publishers.

Borger, Julian. 2018. "Trump administration wants to remove 'gender' from UN human rights documents." *The Guardian* online edition, October 25.

Brah, Avta. 2013. "Pensando En y a Través de La Interseccionalidad." In *Interseccionalidad En Debate. Actas Del Congreso Internacional "Indicadores Interseccionales Y Medidas de Inclusión Social En Instituciones de Educación Superior"*, ed. Martha Zapata Galindo et al., 14-20. Berlin: MISEAL, Freie Universität Berlin.

Brah, Avtar and Ann Phoenix. 2004. "Ain't I a Woman? Revisiting Intersectionality." In *Journal of International Women's Studies* 5, no. 3, 75-86.

Brum, Eliane. 2018. "How a homophobic, misogynist, racist 'thing' could be Brazil's next president." *The Guardian* online edition, October 6.

Butler, Judith. 2015. *Notes Toward a Performative Theory of Assembly*. Cambridge: Harvard University Press.

Butler, Judith. 2019. "The backlash against 'gender ideology' must stop." *The New Statesman America* online edition, January 21.

Caldwell, Kia Lilly. 2007. *Negras in Brazil. Re-envisioning Black Women, Citizenship, and the Politics of Identity*. New Brunswick, New Jersey, and London: Rutgers UP.

Canevari, María Cecilia. 2019. E-mail message to author. April 27.

Canovan, Margaret. 1999. "Trust the People! Populism and the Two Faces of Democracy." *Political Studies* 47, no. 1, 2-16.

Canovan, Margaret. 2002. "Taking Politics to the People: Populism as the Ideology of Democracy." In *Democracies and the Populist Challenge*, ed. Y. Mény and Y. Surel, 25-44. Basingstoke: Palgrave Macmillan.

Cardoso, Rafaela and Margit Ystanes. 2018. "Marielle Franco, Presente!" https://nacla.org/news/2018/03/28/marielle-franco-presente.

Case, Mary Ann. 2019. "Trans Formations in the Vatican's War on 'Gender Ideology'." *Signs: Journal of Women in Culture and Society* 44, no. 3, 639-664.

Clacai. 2018. "Género bajo ataque." https://www.youtube.com/watch?v=wUP5Gu8RgZA.

Cohen, Claire. 2017. "Donald Trump sexism tracker: Every offensive comment in one place." *The Telegraph* online edition, July 14.

Cohen, Stanley. 1981. *Folk Devils and Moral Panics. The Creation of the Mods and Rockers*. New York and London: Routledge.

Combahee River Collective. 1981. "A Black Feminist Statement." In *This Bridge Called My Back: Writings by Radical Women of Color*, ed. Cherrie Moraga and Gloria Anzaldúa, 210-218. New York: Kitchen Table, Women of Color Press.

Coronil, Fernando. 1996. "Beyond Occidentalism: Toward Nonimperial Geohistorical Categories." *Cultural Anthropology* 11, no. 1, 51-87.

Coronil, Fernando. 2011. "The Future in Question: History and Utopia in Latin America (1989-2010)." In *Business as Usual: The Roots of the Global Financial Breakdown* (Possible Futures Series, Vol. 1), ed. Craig Calhoun and Georgi Derluguian, 231-292. New York: New York University Press, SSRC.

Costa, Sérgio. 2018. "Im brasilianischen Wahlkampf ist Verleumdung Programm." *Süddeutsche Zeitung* online edition, October 19.

Crenshaw, Kimberlé. "The Urgency of Intersectionality." https://www.youtube.com/watch?v=akOe5-UsQ2o.

Darlington, Sasha. 2018. "Jair Bolsonaro, Candidate in Brazil, Faces Women's Calls: #NotHim." *The New York Times* online edition, September 24.

Davis, Angela. 1981. *Women, Race, and Class*. New York: Random House.

De Gouges, Olympe. 2003. "Declaration of the Rights of Woman and the Female Citizen." In *The Evolution of International Human Rights: Visions Seen*, ed. Paul Gordon, 18-20. Philadelphia: University of Pennsylvania Press.

Diehl, Paula. 2017. "Why Do Right-Wing Populists Find So Much Appeal in Mass Media?" *The Dahrendorf Forum*. https://www.dahrendorf-forum.eu/why-do-right-wing-populists-find-so-much-appeal-in-mass-media/.

Dietze, Gabriele. 2019. "Why Are Women Attracted to Right-Wing Populism? Sexual Exceptionalism, Emancipation Fatigue, and New Maternalism." In *Right-Wing Populism and Gender: European Perspectives and Beyond*, ed. Gabriele Dietze and Julia Roth, 147-166. Bielefeld: Transcript.

Dietze, Gabriele. 2013. *Weiße Frauen in Bewegung. Genealogien und Konkurrenzen von Race- und Genderpolitiken*. Bielefeld: Transcript.

Dietze, Gabriele. 2015. "Anti-Genderismus intersektional lesen." *Zeitschrift für Medienwissenschaft* 13, no. 2, 125-127.

Dietze, Gabriele. 2016. "Das 'Ereignis' Köln." *Femina Politica* 1, 93-102.

Dietze, Gabriele. 2016b. "Ethnosexismus: Sex-Mob-Narrative um die Kölner Sylvesternacht." *Movements. Journal for Critical Migration and Border Regime Studies* 2, no. 1, 177-185.

Dietze, Gabriele. 2017. *Sexualpolitik: Verflechtungen von Race und Gender*. Frankfurt a.M.: Campus.

Dietze, Gabriele. 2018. "Rechtspopulismus und Geschlecht. Paradox und Leitmotiv." *Femina politica* 27, 34-46.

Dietze, Gabriele, and Julia Roth. 2020. "Right-Wing Populism and Gender: A Preliminary Cartography of an Emergent Field of Research." In *Right-Wing Populism and Gender. European Perspectives and Beyond*, ed. Gabriele Dietze and Julia Roth, 7-21. Bielefeld: Transcript.

Dos Santos, Sonia Beatriz. 2007. "Feminismo Negro Diaspórico." *Gênero* 8, no. 1, 11-26.

Draper, Susana. 2018. "El Paro como Proceso: Construyendo Poéticas de un Nuevo Feminismo." In *8M: Constelación Feminista. ¿Cuál es tu Huelga? ¿Cuál es tu Lucha?*, ed. Verónica Gago et al., 49-72. Buenos Aires: Tinta Limón.

DuBois, Ellen Carol. 2010. "Internationalizing Married Women's Nationality: The Hague Campaign of 1930." In *Globalizing Feminisms, 1789-1945*, ed. Karen Offen, 204-216. London: Routledge.

Duzán, María Jimena. 2018. *Santos: Paradojas de la paz y del poder.* Debate.

EleNão. 2018. "International "Ele Não" Brazilian Women Against Facism – London." https://www.youtube.com/watch?v=0-lHCcBtIVs.

Espinoza, Marcia Vera and Leiza Brumat. 2018. "Brazil elections 2018: how will Bolsonaro's victory affect migration policy in Brazil and South America?" *LSE.* https://blogs.lse.ac.uk/latamcaribbean/2018/10/25/brazil-elections-2018-how-will-a-bolsonaro-victory-affect-migration-policy-in-brazil-and-beyond/.

Fagan Yellin, Jean. 1992. *Women and Sisters: The Antislavery Feminists in American Culture*. New Haven: Yale University Press.

Farris, Sara R. 2012. "Femonationalism and the 'Regular' Army of Labor Called Migrant Women." *History of the Present: A journal of Critical History* 2, no. 2, 184-199.

Farris, Sara R. 2017. *In the Name of Women's Rights: The Rise of Femonationalism.* Durham: Duke University Press.

Fendlay, Cassady. 2019. Interview via skype with Julia Roth. April 3.

Fendlay, Cassady. 2018. Informal talk organized by the Rosa-Luxemburg foundation in Berlin, March 9, 2018, notes by the author and conversation with Cassady Fendlay and the author on the same day.

Fendlay, Cassady. 2018b. Interview by Rosa Luxemburg foundation, Berlin, March 13.

Ferrera, America. 2017. "America Ferrera speaks at Women's March on Washington." *CBS News*. https://www.youtube.com/watch?v=SpdgPTUGFQw.

Francisco, Mônica. 2019. "Marielles Vermächtnis: Herausforderungen für den schwarzen und intersektionalen Feminismus in Brasilien." Paper presented at a conference of Rosa-Luxemburg foundation, Berlin, March 24.

Gago, Verónica et al., eds. 2018. *8M: Constelación Feminista. ¿Cuál es tu huelga? ¿Cuál es tu lucha?* Buenos Aires: Tinta Limón.

Gago, Verónica. 2018. "'#Nosotras Paramos': notas hacía una teoría política de la huelga feminista." In *8M: Constelación Feminista. ¿Cuál es tu huelga? ¿Cuál es tu lucha?*, ed.Verónica Gago et al., 18-19, 22-23. Buenos Aires: Tinta Limón.

Gajanan, Mahita. 2016. "Melania Trump Says Donald's Comments in Leaked Video Were 'Boy Talk'." *Time* online edition, October 17.

Gardels, Nathan. 2018. "Brazil: the latest domino to fall." *The Washington Post* online edition, November 2.

Gay, Roxane. 2018. "After the Start". In *Together We Rise: The Women's March. Behind the Scenes at the Protest Heard around the World,* ed. The Women's March Organizers and Condé Nast, 287-288. New York: HarperCollins.

Goldberg, Michelle. 2019. "The Heartbreak of the 2019 Women's March." *The New York Times* online edition, January 18.

GQ Brazil. 2018. "Antes de Trump, Bolsonaro já se referiu a imigrantes como "escória do mundo." *CQ Brazil* online edition, January 16.

Green, Erica L., Katie Benner and Robert Pear. 2018. "'Transgender' Could Be Defined Out of Existence Under Trump Administration." *The New York Times* online edition, October 21.

Grzebalska, Weronika, Eszter Kováts and Andrea Petö. 2018. "Gender as symbolic glue: How 'gender' became an umbrella term for the rejection of the (neo)liberal order." *Luxemburg Magazine*, 32-37. https://www.zeitschrift-luxemburg.de/lux/wp-content/uploads/2018/09/LUX_Breaking_Feminism_E-Paper.pdf

Gutsche, Elisa, ed. 2018. *Triumph of the Women? The Female Face of the Populist & Far Right in Europe*. Berlin: Friedrich-Ebert-Stiftung.

Hark, Sabine and Paula-Irene Villa, ed. 2015. *Anti-Genderismus. Sexualität und Geschlecht als Schauplätze aktueller politischer Auseinandersetzungen*. Bielefeld: Transcript.

Hark, Sabine and Paula-Irene Villa, eds. 2017. *Unterscheiden und herrschen. Ein Essay zu den ambivalenten Verflechtungen von Rassismus, Sexismus und Feminismus in der Gegenwart*. Bielefeld: Transcript.

Hearn, Jeff. 2011. "Neglected intersectionalities in studying men: Age(ing), virtuality, transnationality." In *Framing Intersectionality: Debates on a Multi-Facetted Concept in Gender Studies*, ed. Helma Lutz, Maria Teresa Herrera Vivar and Linda Supik, 89-104. Farnham: Ashgate.

Hess, Amanda. 2017. "How a Fractious Women's Movement Came to Lead the Left." *The New York Times* online edition, February 7.

Hochschild, Arlie Russell. 2016. *Strangers in their Own Land. Anger and Mourning on the American Right*. New York: The New Press.

Kaiser, Ann Jean. 2018. "'I don't see any reason for feminism': the women backing Brazil's Bolsonaro." *The Guardian* online edition, October 14.

Käufer, Tobias. 2019. "Marielle Franco: Das Gesicht des Widerstands." *Frankfurter Rundschau* online edition, February 19.

Kampwirth, Karen. 2008. "Abortion, Antifeminism, and the Return of Daniel Ortega. In Nicaragua, Leftist Politics?" *Latin American Perspectives* 35 (November), no. 6, 122-136.

Kampwirth, Karen. 2010. "Introduction." In *Gender and Populism in Latin America*, ed. Karen Kampwirth, 1-23. Pennsylvania: Pennsylvania State University Press.

Kendi, Ibram X. 2019. "The Day 'Shithole' Entered the Presidential Lexicon." *The Atlantic* online edition, January 13.

Kilomba, Grada 2019. "The Body as a Political Tool." *Kadist*. https://kadist.org/program/the-body-as-a-political-tool/.

Kish Sklar, Kathryn. 2000. *Women's Rights Emerges within the Antislavery Movement: A Brief History with Documents*. Boston: Bedford, St. Martin's.

Korolczuk, Elżbieta and Agnieszka Graff. 2018. "Gender as 'Ebola from Brussels': The Anticolonial Frame and the Rise of Illiberal Populism." *Signs: Journal of Women in Culture and Society* 43, no. 4, 797-821.

Krastev, Ivan. 2007. "The Populist Moment." *Critique and Humanism* 23, no. 1, 103-108.

Kuhar, Roman and David Paternotte, ed. 2017. *Anti-gender Campaigns in Europe: Mobilizing against Equality*. Lanham: Rowman & Littlefield.

Laclau, Ernesto. 2005. *On Populist Reason*. London, New York: Verso.

LaMalaFe. 2018. "Desmitificando la 'ideología de género' en Colombia." *LaMalaFe*. https://www.lamalafe.lat/desmitificando-la-ideologia-de-genero-en-colombia/.

Lang, Juliane. 2013. "Frauenbilder in der NPD zwischen Modernisierung und traditionellen Vorstellungen." In *Gender und Rechtsextremismusprävention*, ed. Amadeu Antonio Stiftung and Heike Radvan, 89-104. Berlin: Metropol.

Lang, Juliane. 2015. "Mehr als die 'emotionale Kompetenz' der Partei. Mädchen und Frauen in der extremen Rechten." In *Rechter Terror und Rechtsextremismus*, ed. Uwe Wenzel, Beate Rosenzweig and Ulrich Eith, 53-74. Schwalbach: Wochenschau Verlag.

Las Igualadas. 2018. "¿La ideología de género va a homosexualizar a los niños? – Las Igualadas y La Pulla." https://www.youtube.com/watch?time_continue=7&v=qQsv7mS2p8A.

Lavinas, Lena. 2017. "Populism has no side." *Open Democracy*. https://www.opendemocracy.net/en/democraciaabierta/populism-has-no-side/.

Lemons, Gary L. 2009. *Womanist Forefathers: Frederick Douglass and W.E.B. Du Bois*. New York: Suny Press.

Lockward, Alanna. 2013. "Black Europe Body Politics: Towards an Afropean Decolonial Aesthetics." *Social Text*, July 15. https://socialtextjournal.org/periscope_article/black-europe-body-politics-towards-an-afropeandecolonial-aesthetics/.

Lorde, Audre. 1984. "Age, Race, Class and Sex: Women Redefining Difference." In *Sister Outsider: Essays and Speeches*. 114-123. Freedom, CA.: Crossing Press.

Lorey, Isabell. 2019. "'Nicht eine weniger': Die große feministische Streikwelle gegen il/liberale Politiken." Unpublished paper.

Lorey, Isabell. 2019b. "8M – The great feminist strike. Introduction." *Transversal Texts*. https://transversal.at/blog/8m-the-great-feminist-strike.

Lozano Rubello, Gabriela. 2019. "Contra todas las formas de violencia: La lucha de las mujeres Argentinas sigue." *KajaNegra*. http://kajanegra.com/contra-todas-las-formas-de-violencia-la-lucha-de-las-mujeres-argentinas-sigue/.

Lugones, Maria. 2010. "Toward a decolonial feminism." *Hypatia* 25, no. 4, 742-749.

Maihofer, Andrea and Franziska Schutzbach. 2015. "Vom Antifeminismus zum Anti-Genderismus. Eine zeitdiagnostische Betrachtung am Beispiel Schweiz." In *Anti-Genderismus. Sexualität und Geschlecht als Schauplätze aktueller politischer Auseinandersetzun-*

gen, ed. Sabine Hark and Paula-Irene Villa, 201-217. Bielefeld: Transcript.

McClintock, Anne. 1995. *Imperial Leather: Race, Class and Sexuality in the Colonial Context*. New York: Routledge.

McLoughlin, Beth. 2019. "Brazil's Trump? A congressman with presidential ambitions is being compared to Donald Trump. Can he win?" *U.S. News* online edition, January 19.

Mepschen, Paul and Jan Willem Duyvendak. 2012. "European Sexual Nationalisms. The Culturalization of Citizenship and the sexual Politics of Belonging and Exclusion." *Perspectives on Europe* 42, no. 1, 70-76.

Mirza, Heidi. 2013. "'A second skin': Embodied intersectionality, transnationalism and narratives of identity and belonging among Muslim women in Britain." *Women's Studies International Forum* 36 (January-February), 5-15.

Mitchell, Amy, Katarina Eva Matsa, Jeffrey Gottfried, Galen Stocking and Elizabeth Grieco. 2017. "Covering President Trump in a Polarized Media Environment." *Pew Research Center. Journalism & Media*. http://www.journalism.org/2017/10/02/covering-president-trump-in-a-polarized-media-environment.

Molloy, David. 2018. "What is populism, and what does the term actually mean?" *BBC News* online edition, March 6.

Morrison, Matt. 2018. "Why are these women sticking with Trump?" *BBC News* online edition, January 18.

Mouffe, Chantal. 2018. *Für einen linken Populismus*. Frankfurt a.M.: Edition Suhrkamp.

Moynagh, Maureen Anne. 2012. "Volume Introduction: Transnational Collaborations and Crosscurrents." In *Documenting First Wave Feminisms. Volume I: Transnational Collaborations and Crosscurrents*, ed. Nancy Margaret Forestell and Maureen Anne Moynagh, 3-16. Toronto: UP of Toronto.

Mudde, Cass. 2004. "The Populist Zeitgeist." *Government and Opposition* 39, no. 4, 541-563.

Mudde, Cass and Cristóbal Rovira Kaltwasser. 2013. "Exclusionary vs. Inclusionary Populism: Comparing Contemporary Europe and Latin America." *Government and Opposition* 48, no. 2, 147-174.

Mudde, Cass and Cristóbal Rovira Kaltwasser. 2017. *Populism: A Very Short Introduction*. New York: Oxford University Press.

Muzi, Carolina. 2018. "La historia del pañuelo verde: cómo surgió el emblema del nuevo feminismo en Argentina." *InfoBae* online edition, August 5.

Ni Una Menos. 2015. "Manifiestos." http://niunamenos.org.ar/manifiestos/3-de-junio-2015/.

Ninja, Mídia. 2018. "Gerechtigkeit für Marielle Franco." *Amnesty International*. https://www.amnesty.de/gerechtigkeit-fuer-marielle-franco.

Obama, Barack. 2016. "Glamour Exclusive: President Barack Obama Says, 'This Is What a Feminist Looks Like'." *Glamour* online edition, August 4.

Owen, Diana. 2018. "The New Media's Role in Politics." *BBVA Open Mind*. https://www.bbvaopenmind.com/en/articles/the-new-media-s-role-in-politics/.

Paris, Francesca. 2019. "Brazilian President Bolsonaro Withdraws from U.N. Compact on Migration." *NPR* online edition, January 9.

Pelinka, Anton. 2002. "Die FPÖ in der vergleichenden Parteienforschung. Zur typologischen Einordnung der Freiheitlichen Partei Österreichs." *Österreichische Zeitschrift für Politikwissenschaft* 31, no. 3, 281-290.

Pelizzon, Sheila. 1998. "But can she spin? The decline in the social standing of women in the transition from feudalism to capitalism." PhD diss, State University of New York at Binghamton.

Pelizzon, Sheila. 2002. "Writing on Gender in World-Systems Perspective." In *The Modern/Colonial/Capitalist World-System in the Twentieth Century: Global Processes, Antisystemic Movements, and the Geopolitics of Knowledge*, ed. Ramón Grosfoguel and Ana Margarita Cervantes-Rodríguez, 199-212. Westport: Greenwood Press.

Perry, Keisha-Khan Y. 2009. "'The Groundings With My Sisters': Toward a Black Diasporic Feminist Agenda in the Americas." *The*

Scholar and Feminist Online 7.2 (spring). http://sfonline.barnard.edu/africana/perry_01.htm.

Petö, Andrea. 2018. "Without Remedy: Lessons Learned from a Gendered Analysis of the 2018 Hungarian General Elections." *Femina politica* 2, 152-158.

Phillips, Dom. 2018. "Bolsonaro to abolish human rights ministry in favour of family values." *The Guardian* online edition, September 10.

Poo, Ai-Jen. 2018. "A Woman's Work is Never Done (in a Democracy)." In *Together We Rise: The Women's March. Behind the Scenes at the Protest Heard around the World*, ed. The Women's March Organizers and Condé Nast, 69-72. New York: HarperCollins.

Prandini Assis, Mariana and Ana Carolina Ogando. 2018. "Gender Ideology and the Brazilian Elections." *Public Seminar*. http://www.publicseminar.org/2018/11/gender-ideology-and-the-brazilian-elections/.

Pratt, Mary Louise. 1992. *Imperial Eyes: Travel Writing and Transculturation*. London, New York: Routledge.

Puar, Jasbir K. 2007. *Terrorist Assemblages: Homonationalism in Queer Times*. Durham, London: Duke University Press.

Pussyhat Project. 2020. "Pussyhat Project TM. Design interventions for social change." https://www.pussyhatproject.com.

Randeria, Shalini. 1999. "Jenseits von Soziologie und soziokultureller Anthropologie: Zur Ortsbestimmung der nichtwestlichen Welt in einer zukünftigen Sozialtheorie." *Soziale Welt* 50, no. 1, 373-382.

Randeria, Shalini. 2006. "Entangled histories of uneven modernities: Civil society, caste solidarities and legal pluralism in post-colonial India." In *Civil Society – Berlin Perspectives*, ed. John Keane, 213-242. New York: Berghahn.

Redecker, Eva von. 2017. "Vier Thesen zum Zusammenhang von Rechtspopulismus und Anti-Genderismus (und eine halbe zu deren Überwindung)." *CTB Critical Theory in Berlin*. http://criticaltheoryinberlin.de/wp-content/uploads/2017/04/Antigenderismus_4_Thesen. pdf.

Reisigl, Martin. 2012. "Zur kommunikativen Dimension des Rechtspopulismus." In *Populismus. Herausforderung oder Gefahr für die*

Demokratie?, ed. Sir Peter Ustinov Institut, 141-162. Wien: New Academic Press.

Resumen Latinoamericano. 2019. "Argentina. Resumen gremial y social. Llamamiento al paro feminista 8M 2019/ Crece la desigualdad en la Ciudad y aumenta la indigencia entre los menores de 15 años/ Panorama político-sindical: Inflación y despidos en ascenso (Más información)." http://www.resumenlatinoamericano.org/2019/03/03/argentina-resumen-gremial-y-social-llamamiento-al-paro-feminista-8m-2019-crece-la-desigualdad-en-la-ciudad-y-aumenta-la-indigencia-entre-los-menores-de-15-anos-panorama-politico-sindical-inflacio/.

Rhodan, Maya. 2016. "President Obama at Women's Summit: This Is What a Feminist Looks Like." *Time* online edition, June 14.

Roberts, Nigel. 2018. "Brazil's New Racist President Has Anti-Black Agenda." *News One* online edition, October 29.

Roth, Benita. 2004. *Separate Roads to Feminism: Black, Chicana and White Feminists in America's Second Wave*. Cambridge: Cambridge University Press.

Roth, Julia. 2013. "Entangled Inequalities as Intersectionalities: Towards an Epistemic Sensibilization." *desiguALdades.net Working Paper Series* no. 43, Berlin.

Roth, Julia. 2014. *Lateinamerikas koloniales Gedächtnis. Vom Ende der Ressourcen, so wie wir sie kennen*. Baden Baden: Nomos.

Roth, Julia. 2016. "Feminist Politics of Connectedness in the Americas." In *Politics of Entanglements in the Americas*, ed. Jochen Kemner und Lukas Rehm, 73-96. Trier: WVT.

Roth, Julia. 2018. "Feminism Otherwise: Intersectionality beyond Occidentalism." *InterDisciplines* 2, 97-122.

Roth, Julia. 2019. "'Manifiesto De Solidaridad Continental' Alliances and Inequalities: Inter-American Feminist Networks 1840-1948." *Comparative American Studies* 14, no. 3-4, 204-220.

Roth, Julia and Manuela Boatcă. 2016. "Staatsbürgerschaft, Gender und globale Ungleichheiten." *Feministische Studien* 34, no. 2, 189-206.

Rubin, Gayle. 1984. "Thinking Sex: Notes for a Radical Theory of the Politics of Sexuality." In *Pleasure and Danger: Exploring Female Sexuality*, ed. Carole S. Vance, 267-293. London: Pandora.

Salam, Maya. 2018. "They Challenged the Status Quo. On Tuesday, They'll Find Out Who's With Them." *The New York Times* online edition, November 2.

Sauer, Birgit. 2013. "Intersectionality From Above – Framing Muslim Headscarves in European Policy Debates." Paper presented at the ECPR General Conference Sciences Po, Bordeaux, September 4-7.

Sauer, Birgit. 2017. "Gesellschaftstheoretische Überlegungen zum europäischen Rechtspopulismus. Zum Erklärungspotenzial der Kategorie Geschlecht." *Politische Vierteljahresschrift* 58, no. 1, 1-20.

Scott, Eugene. 2018. "Trump says he rejects feminism because he is 'for everyone'." *The Washington Post* online edition, January 28.

Seeßlen, Georg. 2017. *Trump! POPulismus als Politik*. Berlin: Bertz + Fischer Verlag.

Senra, Ricardo. 2018. "Jair Bolsonaro: la verdadera identidad de la 'brasileña negra y pobre' del polémico video difundido por el candidato a la presidencia de Brasil." *BBC News Brazil* online edition, September 21.

Shear, Michael D. and Maggie Haberman. 2019. "For Trump, Brazil's President Is Like Looking in the Mirror." *The New York Times* online edition, March 19.

Shepherd, Verene. 2008. "Women and the Abolition Campaign in the African Atlantic." *Journal of Caribbean History* 42, no. 1, 131-153.

Shepherd, Verene. 2011. *Engendering Caribbean History: Cross-Cultural Perspectives*. Kingston: Ian Randle Publishers.

Shepherd, Verene, Bridget Brereton, and Barbara Bailey. 1995. *Engendering History: Caribbean Women in Historical Perspective*. Kingston: Ian Randle Publishers.

Shohat, Ella. 2006. *Taboo Memories: Diasporic Voices*. Durham and London: Duke University Press.

Sosa, Joseph Jay. 2019. "Subversive, Mother, Killjoy: Sexism against Dilma Rousseff and the Social Imaginary of Brazil's Rightward

Turn." *Signs: Journal of Women in Culture and Society* 44, no. 3, 717-741.

Spierings, Niels and Andrej Zaslove. 2015. "Gendering the vote for populist radical-right parties." *Patterns of Prejudice* 49, no. 1-2 (Special issue: Gender and Populist Radical Right Politics), 135-162.

Spivak, Gayatri Chakravorty. 1988. *Can the Subaltern Speak?* New York and London: Routledge.

Spivak, Gayatri Chakravorty. 1989. *In Other Worlds: Essays in Cultural Politics*. New York: Routledge.

Stanley Holten, Sandra. 2010. "To educate women into rebellion Elizabeth Cady Stanton and the creation of a transatlantic network of radical suffragists." In *Globalizing Feminisms, 1789-1945*, ed. Karen Offen, 36-50. London: Routledge.

Stegemann, Bernd. 2017. *Das Gespenst des Populismus. Ein Essay zur politischen Dramaturgie*. Berlin: Theater der Zeit.

Strick, Simon. 2019. "The Alternative Right, Masculinities, and Quotidian Affect." Unpublished paper.

Süddeutsche Zeitung. 2017. "Wie hält Trump es mit dem Glauben?" *Süddeutsche Zeitung* online edition, May 21.

Suh, Krista. 2018. "How could I predict how many hats would be there?" In *Together We Rise: The Women's March. Behind the Scenes at the Protest Heard around the World*, ed. The Women's March Organizers and Condé Nast, 57. New York: HarperCollins.

Taggart, P. 2000. *Populism*. Buckingham: Open University Press.

Telesur. 2018. "Bolsonaro Abolishes Human Rights Ministry For 'Family Values'." *Telesur English* online edition, December 7.

The Daily Mail. 2018. "Tropical Trump: The similarities between U.S. President and Brazil's far-right frontrunner." *The Daily Mail* online edition, October 30.

The Women's March Organizers and Condé Nast (WMO). 2018. *Together We Rise: The Women's March. Behind the Scenes at the Protest Heard around the World.* New York: HarperCollins.

Tisdall, Simon. 2018. "Donald Trump's war with the media has deadly implications." *The Guardian* online edition, August 4.

Truth, Sojourner. 1851. "Ain't I a Woman." In *Wikisource*. https://en.wikisource.org/wiki/Ain't_I_a_Woman%3F.

Uchoa, Pablo. 2018. "Jair Bolsonaro: Why Brazilian women are saying #NotHim." *BBC News* online edition, September 21.

Vacca, Celina. 2017. "Un nuevo lenguaje que invita a poner el cuerpo." In *#NiUnaMenos. Vivxs nos queremos*, 39-41. Buenos Aires: Milena Caserola.

Vargas, José Antonio. 2018. "How to be an Ally." In *Together We Rise: The Women's March. Behind the Scenes at the Protest Heard around the World*, ed. The Women's March Organizers and Condé Nast, 91-93. New York: HarperCollins.

Varias autoras. 2017. *#NiUnaMenos. Vivxs nos queremos*. Buenos Aires: Milena Caserola.

Viveros Vigoya, Mara. 2013. "Movilidades y desigualdades espaciales y sociales en el contexto del multiculturalismo latinoamericano. Una lectura en clave de género." In *Espacios de género. Adlaf Congreso Anual 2012*, ed. Juliana Ströbele Gregor and Dörte Wollrad, 189-203. Buenos Aires: Nueva Sociedad, Fundación Friedrich Ebert, Adlaf.

Wade, Peter. 2009. *Race and Sex in Latin America*. London: Pluto Press.

Walters, Joanna. 2017. "What is Daca and who are the Dreamers?" *The Guardian* online edition, September 14.

Watson, Katy. 2018. "'Feminism is sexist': The women backing Brazil's Bolsonaro." *BBC News* online edition, October 23.

Wiegel, Gerd. 2018. "Holy Shit. Gender as a unifying theme for the Right." *Luxemburg. Gesellschaftsanalyse und politische Praxis*, 38-43. https://www.zeitschrift-luxemburg.de/holy-shit-gender-as-a-unifying -theme-for-the-right/.

Wilson, Jamia. 2018. "Introduction." In *Together We Rise: The Women's March. Behind the Scenes at the Protest Heard around the World*, ed. The Women's March Organizers and Condé Nast, 13-16. New York: HarperCollins.

Wollstonecraft, Mary. 2004. *A Vindication on the Rights of Women.* New York: Penguin Classics.

The Women's March Organizers. 2018. "Preface." In *Together We Rise: The Women's March. Behind the Scenes at the Protest Heard around the World*, ed. The Women's March Organizers and Condé Nast, 11-12. New York: Harper Collins.

Women's March. 2019. "Women's Agenda." In *Women's March.* https://womensmarch.com/agenda.

Worley, Will. 2017. "Donald Trump 'reduced Ivanka to tears' by refusing to apologise fully for 'grabbing women' comments." *The Independent* online edition, May 2.

Yuval-Davis, Nira. 1997. *Gender and Nation.* London: Sage.

Yuval-Davis, Nira. 2007. "Intersectionality, Citizenship and Contemporary Politics of Belonging." *Critical review of International, Social and Political Philosophy* 10, no. 4, 561-574.

Yuval-Davis, Nira, Georgie Wemyss, and Kathryn Cassidy. 2018. "Everyday Bordering, Belonging and the Reorientation of British Immigration Legislation." *Sociology* 52, no. 2, 228-244.

Zakaria, Fareed. 1997. "The Rise of Illiberal Democracy." *Foreign Affairs* 76, no. 6, 22-43.

Zapata Galindo, Martha. 2011. *El Paradigma de La Interseccionalidad En América Latina.* [Lecture given at the Lateinamerika-Institut of the Freie Universität Berlin November 17, 2011, notes taken by the author.]

Zurcher, Anthony. 2018. "Why Donald Trump attacks the media." *BBC News* online edition, July 21.

INTER-AMERICAN STUDIES
Cultures – Societies – History

ESTUDIOS INTERAMERICANOS
Culturas – Sociedades – Historia

This interdisciplinary series examines national and transnational issues in the cultures, societies, and histories of the Americas. It creates a forum for a critical academic dialogue between North and South, promoting an inter-American paradigm that shifts the scholarly focus from methodological nationalism to the wider context of the Western Hemisphere.

Vol. 1
Raab, Josef, Sebastian Thies, and Daniela Noll-Opitz, eds. *Screening the Americas: Narration of Nation in Documentary Film / Proyectando las Américas: Narración de la nación en el cine documental.* 2011. 470 pp.

WVT Wissenschaftlicher Verlag Trier	ISBN 978-3-86821-331-7	€ 29,50
Bilingual Press / Editorial Bilingüe	ISBN 978-1-931010-83-2	$ 29.50

Vol. 2
Raussert, Wilfried, and Michelle Habell-Pallán, eds. *Cornbread and Cuchifritos: Ethnic Identity Politics, Transnationalization, and Transculturation in American Urban Popular Music.* 2011. 292 pp.

WVT Wissenschaftlicher Verlag Trier	ISBN 978-3-86821-265-5	€ 29,50
Bilingual Press / Editorial Bilingüe	ISBN 978- 1-931010-80-1	$ 29.50

Vol. 3
Butler, Martin, Jens Martin Gurr, and Olaf Kaltmeier, eds. *EthniCities: Metropolitan Cultures and Ethnic Identities in the Americas.* 2011. 268 pp.

WVT Wissenschaftlicher Verlag Trier	ISBN 978-3-86821-310-2	€ 29,50
Bilingual Press / Editorial Bilingüe	ISBN 978-1-931010-81-8	$ 29.50

Vol. 4
Gurr, Jens Martin, and Wilfried Raussert, eds. *Cityscapes in the Americas and Beyond: Representations of Urban Complexity in Literature and Film.* 2011. 300 pp.

WVT Wissenschaftlicher Verlag Trier	ISBN 978-3-86821-324-9	€ 29,50
Bilingual Press / Editorial Bilingüe	ISBN 978-1-931010-82-5	$ 29.50

Vol. 5

Kirschner, Luz Angélica, ed. *Expanding* Latinidad*: An Inter-American Perspective.* 2012. 292 pp.

WVT Wissenschaftlicher Verlag Trier	ISBN 978-3-86821-309-6	€ 29,50
Bilingual Press / Editorial Bilingüe	ISBN 978-1-931010-84-9	$ 29.50

Vol. 6

Raussert, Wilfried, and Graciela Martínez-Zalce, eds. *(Re)Discovering 'America': Road Movies and Other Travel Narratives in North America / (Re)Descubriendo 'América': Road movie y otras narrativas de viaje en América del Norte*. 2012. 252 pp.

WVT Wissenschaftlicher Verlag Trier	ISBN 978-3-86821-384-3	€ 29,50
Bilingual Press / Editorial Bilingüe	ISBN 978-1-931010-91-7	$ 29.50

Vol. 7

Kaltmeier, Olaf, ed. *Transnational Americas: Envisioning Inter-American Area Studies in Globalization Processes*. 2013. 278 pp.

WVT Wissenschaftlicher Verlag Trier	ISBN 978-3-86821-415-4	€ 29,50
Bilingual Press / Editorial Bilingüe	ISBN 978-1-931010-92-4	$ 29.50

Vol. 8

Raab, Josef, and Alexander Greiffenstern, eds. *Interculturalism in North America: Canada, the United States, Mexico, and Beyond.* 2013. 312 pp.

WVT Wissenschaftlicher Verlag Trier	ISBN 978-3-86821-460-4	€ 29,50
Bilingual Press / Editorial Bilingüe	ISBN 978-1-931010-99-3	$ 29.50

Vol. 9

Raab, Josef, ed. *New World Colors: Ethnicity, Belonging, and Difference in the Americas*. 2014. 418 pp.

WVT Wissenschaftlicher Verlag Trier	ISBN 978-3-86821-461-1	€ 29,50
Bilingual Press / Editorial Bilingüe	ISBN 978-1-939743-00-8	$ 39.50

Vol. 10

Roth, Julia. *Occidental Readings, Decolonial Practices: A Selection on Gender, Genre, and Coloniality in the Americas*. 2014. 284 pp.

WVT Wissenschaftlicher Verlag Trier	ISBN 978-3-86821-446-8	€ 26,50
Bilingual Press / Editorial Bilingüe	ISBN 978-1-939743-07-7	$ 32.50

Vol. 11

Thies, Sebastian, Gabriele Pisarz-Ramirez, and Luzelena Gutiérrez de Velasco, eds. *Of Fatherlands and Motherlands: Gender and Nation in the Americas / De Patrias y Matrias: Género y nación en las Américas*. 2015. 344 pp.

WVT Wissenschaftlicher Verlag Trier	ISBN 978-3-86821-528-1	€ 29,50
Bilingual Press / Editorial Bilingüe	ISBN 978-1-939743-08-4	$ 39.50

Vol. 12

Fuchs, Rebecca. *Caribbeanness as a Global Phenomenon: Junot Díaz, Edwidge Danticat, and Cristina García*. 2014. 298 pp.

WVT Wissenschaftlicher Verlag Trier	ISBN 978-3-86821-533-5	€ 26,50
Bilingual Press / Editorial Bilingüe	ISBN 978-1-939743-09-1	$ 32.50

Vol. 13

Andres, Julia. *¡Cuéntame algo! – Chicana Narrative Beyond the Borderlands*. 2015. 202 pp.

WVT Wissenschaftlicher Verlag Trier	ISBN 978-3-86821-569-4	€ 25,00
Bilingual Press / Editorial Bilingüe	ISBN 978-1-939743-11-4	$ 28.50

Vol. 14

Hertlein, Saskia. *Tales of Transformation: Emerging Adulthood, Migration, and Ethnicity in Contemporary American Literature*. 2014. 228 pp.

WVT Wissenschaftlicher Verlag Trier	ISBN 978-3-86821-570-0	€ 25,00
Bilingual Press / Editorial Bilingüe	ISBN 978-1-939743-10-7	$ 31.50

Vol. 15

Raab, Josef, and Saskia Hertlein, eds. *Spaces – Communities – Discourses: Charting Identity and Belonging in the Americas*. 2016. 382 pp.

WVT Wissenschaftlicher Verlag Trier	ISBN 978-3-86821-590-8	€ 29,50
Bilingual Press / Editorial Bilingüe	ISBN 978-1-939743-13-8	$ 39.50

Vol. 16

Mehring, Frank, ed. *The Mexico Diary: Winold Reiss between Vogue Mexico and Harlem Renaissance. An Illustrated Trilingual Edition with Commentary and Musical Interpretation* (includes color plates and audio CD). 2016. 244 pp.

WVT Wissenschaftlicher Verlag Trier	ISBN 978-3-86821-594-6	€ 29,50
Bilingual Press / Editorial Bilingüe	ISBN 978-1-939743-14-5	$ 39.50

Vol. 17

Raussert, Wilfried, Brian Rozema, Yolanda Campos, and Marius Littschwager, eds. *Key Tropes in Inter-American Studies: Perspectives from the* forum for inter-american research (fiar). 2015. 374 pp.

WVT Wissenschaftlicher Verlag Trier	ISBN 978-3-86821-627-1	€ 29,50
Bilingual Press / Editorial Bilingüe	ISBN 978-1-939743-16-9	$ 39.50

Vol. 19

Rehm, Lukas, Jochen Kemner, and Olaf Kaltmeier, eds. *Politics of Entanglement in the Americas: Connecting Transnational Flows and Local Perspectives*. 2017. 226 pp.

WVT Wissenschaftlicher Verlag Trier	ISBN 978-3-86821-675-2	€ 27,50
Bilingual Press / Editorial Bilingüe	ISBN 978-1-939743-17-6	$ 32.50

Vol. 20

Britt Arredondo, Christopher. *Imperial Idiocy: A Reflection on Forced Displacement in the Americas*. 2017. 194 pp.

WVT Wissenschaftlicher Verlag Trier	ISBN 978-3-86821-706-3	€ 26,50
Bilingual Press / Editorial Bilingüe	ISBN 978-1-939743-20-6	$ 30.00

Vol. 21

Schemien, Alexia. *Of Virgins, Curanderas, and Wrestler Saints: Un/Doing Religion in Contemporary Mexican American Literature*. 2018. 218 pp.

WVT Wissenschaftlicher Verlag Trier	ISBN 978-3-86821-724-7	€ 27,50
Bilingual Press / Editorial Bilingüe	ISBN 978-1-939743-22-0	$ 32.50

Vol. 22

Fulger, Maria Diana. *The Cuban Post-Socialist Exotic: Contemporary U.S. American Travel Narratives about Cuba.* 2020. 266 pp.

WVT Wissenschaftlicher Verlag Trier	ISBN 978-3-86821-769-8	€ 32,50
Bilingual Press / Editorial Bilingüe	ISBN 978-1-939743-27-5	$ 36.00

Vol. 24

Kaltmeier, Olaf, Mirko Petersen, Wilfried Raussert, and Julia Roth, eds. *Cherishing the Past, Envisioning the Future. Entangled Practises of Heritage and Utopia in the Americas.* 2021. 176 pp.

WVT Wissenschaftlicher Verlag Trier	ISBN 978-3-86821-804-6	€ 23,50
UNO University of New Orleans Press	ISBN 978-1-60801-206-0	$ 27.50

Vol. 26

Raussert, Wilfried. *'What's Going On': How Music Shapes the Social.* 2021. 224 pp.

WVT Wissenschaftlicher Verlag Trier	ISBN 978-3-86821-811-4	€ 28,50
UNO University of New Orleans Press	ISBN 978-1-60801-199-5	$ 34.00

Vol. 27

Frank-Job, Barbara. *Immigration as a Process: Temporality Concepts in Blogs of Latin American Immigrants to Québec.* 2021. 138 pp.

WVT Wissenschaftlicher Verlag Trier	ISBN 978-3-86821-820-6	€ 20,00
UNO University of New Orleans Press	ISBN 978-1-60801-215-2	$ 24.00

Vol. 28

Roth, Julia. *Can Feminism Trump Populism? Right-Wing Trends and Intersectional Contestations in the Americas.* 2021. 166 pp.

WVT Wissenschaftlicher Verlag Trier	ISBN 978-3-86821-821-3	€ 23,00
UNO University of New Orleans Press	ISBN 978-1-60801-205-3	$ 26.00

Vol. 30
Buitrago Valencia, Clara. *Missionaries: Migrants or Expatriates? Guatemalan Pentecostal Leaders in Los Angeles.* 2021. 236 pp.
WVT Wissenschaftlicher Verlag Trier ISBN 978-3-86821-818-3 € 28,50
UNO University of New Orleans Press ISBN 978-1-60801-210-7 $ 34.50

Vol. 31
Schwabe, Nicole. *De-Centering History Education: Creating Knowledge of Global Entanglements.* 2021. 92 pp.
WVT Wissenschaftlicher Verlag Trier ISBN 978-3-86821-828-2 € 18,00
UNO University of New Orleans Press ISBN 978-1-60801-214-5 $ 21.00

Vol. 32
Manke, Albert. *Coping with Discrimination and Exclusion. Experiences of Free Chinese Migrants in the Americas in a Transregional and Diachronic Perspective.* 2021. 162 pp.
WVT Wissenschaftlicher Verlag Trier ISBN 978-3-86821-829-9 € 23,00
UNO University of New Orleans Press ISBN 978-1-60801-207-7 $ 27.00

Vol. 33
Rohland, Eleonora. *Entangled Histories and the Environment? Socio-Environmental Transformations in the Caribbean, 1492-1800.* 2021. 92 pp.
WVT Wissenschaftlicher Verlag Trier ISBN 978-3-86821-833-6 € 18,00
UNO University of New Orleans Press ISBN 978-1-60801-208-4 $ 21.00

Vol. 34
Kaltmeier, Olaf. *National Parks from North to South. An Entangled History of Conservation and Colonization in Argentina.* 2021. 210 pp.
WVT Wissenschaftlicher Verlag Trier ISBN 978-3-86821-834-3 € 27,50
UNO University of New Orleans Press ISBN 978-1-60801-204-6 $ 32.50

Vol. 35
Raussert, Wilfried. *Off the Grid. Art Practices and Public Space.* 2021. 232 pp.
WVT Wissenschaftlicher Verlag Trier ISBN 978-3-86821-835-0 € 29,50
UNO University of New Orleans Press ISBN 978-1-60801-213-8 $ 34.50

Vol. 36
Ravasio, Paola. *This Train Is Not Bound to Glory. A Study of Literary Trainscapes.* 2021. 114 pp.
WVT Wissenschaftlicher Verlag Trier ISBN 978-3-86821-836-7 € 18,00
UNO University of New Orleans Press ISBN 978-1-60801-216-9 $ 21.00

Vol. 37

Schäfer, Heinrich Wilhelm. *Protestant 'Sects' and the Spirit of (Anti-)Imperialism. Religious Entanglements in the Americas.* 2021. 242 pp.

WVT Wissenschaftlicher Verlag Trier	ISBN 978-3-86821-855-9	€ 29,50
UNO University of New Orleans Press	ISBN 978-1-60801-209-1	$ 34.50